DREAM ON

OVERCOMING ADVERSITIES TO FULFILL YOUR LIFE'S DREAMS

RICHIE MULLIS

DREAM ON
Overcoming Adversities to Fulfill Your Life's Dreams
By Richie Mullis

Published by Blaze Publishing House
www.blazepublishinghouse.com
BPH is a division of Ministry Solutions, LLC
Mansfield, TX 76063
info@BlazePublishingHouse.com

Unless otherwise indicated, all Scripture quotations in this volume are taken from the Holy Bible, *New King James Version*, Copyright © 1982 by Thomas Nelson, Inc. Used by permission. All rights reserved.

Manuscript Development by Kent Booth
Editing and Interior Design by Laura-Lee Booth
Cover Design by Steve John at Emphasis Productions
emphasisproduction@gmail.com
Cover Photography by Hello Heart Photography
Prepared for Publication by Ministry Solutions, LLC

ISBN-10: 0-9825289-6-5
ISBN-13: 978-0-9825289-6-9

BPH

This book is dedicated to my life hero, my dad, Donnie Mullis.

You showed me how to be a man.
Your hard work and provision for our family still amazes me today.
You taught me that hard work and determination always pays off.
You taught me how to take care of my family.
I hope I always make you proud until I see you one day again.
I honor you with this book.

What Others are Saying . . .

"All people have a dream and a few see that dream come to fruition, but in his new book, *Dream On*, Richie Mullis gives clear and applicable steps for achieving your dream. This is one of those books that is well worth the time spent to read. *Dream On!*"

Bishop Jim Bolin
Founding and Senior Pastor, Trinity Chapel Church of God
Powder Springs, GA

"Richie Mullis is one of the most focused individuals I have ever met. His passion to reach people and give them hope has been inspiring to me personally for years. *Dream On* is a must-read book, if you're ready to tackle ANYTHING that stands between you and your God-given purpose."

Pastor Trent Cory
International Recording Artist/Minister/Songwriter

"*Dream On*. What a tremendous title! If there is anything our Father God wants us to do is dream and dream big. Richie Mullis has done just that. Not only has he seen his dreams come to fruition, he also knows there's always more. *Dream On* is a book that you can't put down, written by an on-time pastor who is anointed and blessed mightily by the Holy Spirit. His revelation and life experiences will challenge you to dream more in your own life."

Dr. Steve L. Brock
International Evangelist

"My friend, Richie Mullis, has provided a tremendous resource for all audiences. Richie's wording, Biblical teaching, and life applications will be an encouragement to readers of all ages. Whether you have a love for reading or you're a casual reader, this book will keep your attention and install a greater wisdom for your current place in life. Morre importantly, it will motivate you to dream where God has destined for you to go."

Richie Hughes
Author of _Start Here, Go Anywhere_

"There are rare moments in life when you are given a gift that leaves you with a passionate and relentless drive to pursue life with such promise and purpose—to dream! Yet, that is the gift you are given in the pages of this incredible book. The wisdom, insight, and life-proven principles are shared by Richie Mullis in _Dream On_. This is a masterpiece and a must-read for those who are tired of living the status quo or simply desire to better understand the potential of fulfilling the dream that God has reserved with your name on it! Your life will never be the same."

Barry Clardy
Senior Pastor, Princeton Pike Church of God
Hamilton, OH

"Richie Mullis is a man on a mission. Few men I've ever met have been more driven, determined, and decisive about walking out and following the plan God has put in their heart. Richie has fearlessly followed the dream. Inside of these pages, you will learn the secrets how, like Richie, you can walk out the dream God has for your life. Get ready to live your dreams."

Joel Scrivner
Pastor, Covenant Church
McKinney, TX
Author of _The Supernatural You_

"Relevant, revolutionary, cutting edge, and life changing describes Richie Mullis' book, *Dream On*. Using personal experiences combined with the truth of God's Word, Richie reveals that the dream in you is big, real, and God's perfect plan for your life. It's a must-read for everyone!"

Judy Jacobs
Pastor, Author, Worshiper

"I love this book, *Dream On*! In its pages, Richie Mullis goes to great extremes to encourage you that through Christ and His anointing in your life, you can reach your highest goals and see the dream in you fulfilled. This book is a game changer! Read, reach, and receive."

Jamie Tuttle
Senior Pastor, Dwelling Place Church International
Cleveland, TN

"Dreamers think, act, and talk differently than others. Dreamers do not let the status quo stop them from accomplishing their dream. There will always be dream discouragers and dream killers. Caleb, one of the twelve Old Testament men who were sent to spy out the Promised Land, could have let his dream die. But, in fact, forty-five years after his generation rejected his report, he challenged Joshua with these words: 'Here I am this day, eighty-five years old. I am strong for war. Now, give me this mountain!' Caleb didn't allow the dream to die, but believed and embraced the dream until it became reality. In his book, Richie Mullis demonstrates through real life experiences and practical wisdom how you can see your dreams come true. Strap on your seat belt and get ready to *Dream On*!"

Jim Milligan
Senior Pastor, The Ministry Center
Chattanooga, TN

"Richie Mulls is a rock-solid family man and engaging teacher. He is absolutely passionate about reaching others with God's promise of salvation. His new book is timely and undoubtedly Spirit-directed. I know you'll really enjoy the principles shared in *Dream On*."

Tony Brock, Senior Pastor
Hope and Life Fellowship
Snellville, GA

ACKNOWLEDGMENTS

To Leann, my wife, mother of our three children, and my life partner. Your unconditional love and support throughout our ministry has been an amazing model for our three daughters. You are truly a gift to so many.

To my girls, Sydni, Ashtyn, and Eden. You will never know how special you are to Daddy. Read this book, and let it be a reminder to dare to dream the impossible and to never ever give up on those dreams!

To our great church, FreeLife, which I have the privilege of pastoring. Thank you for allowing me to dream. I pray that I always challenge you to dream and be all that God has called you to be. I am honored to be called your pastor.

To my Lord and Savior, Jesus Christ. I thank You for never giving up on me and standing by me every step of the journey. You have been my Provider, Healer, Protector, Peace-speaker, and mighty Comforter during the darkest seasons of my life. I will love You forever.

CONTENTS

Foreword by Mike Hayes 13

Chapter 1   Calling all Dreamers 15

Chapter 2   Two Simple Words 29

Chapter 3   Press On! 43

Chapter 4   The Miracle of Emptiness 57

Chapter 5   Stirring the Waters 73

Chapter 6   Divine Counterbalance 95

Chapter 7   Passing the Test 111

Chapter 8   The Process of a Dream 135

Chapter 9   The Power of Potential 153

Chapter 10   Signs of Grace 165

FOREWORD

By Mike Hayes

M y friend, Richie Mullis, has taken on the monumental task of writing a book. Talk about a dream! As an author myself, I can tell you that writing a book is a painful, but rewarding, process. Then, to take on the subject of fulfilling your life-dreams is even more challenging. Why? Because it carries so much weight. Buried deep within the DNA of every one of us is that drive to somehow fulfill the purpose for our existence. Every dream is important, mainly because of the potential outcome for the good of humanity. Whether it's how to build a better mousetrap or the cure for cancer, the fulfilling of your God-given dream has the potential to affect lives around the world for generations to come.

Dream On will sort out the details of how to discover, develop, and walk out your life-dream. As unique as your fingerprint is the God-given dream that was in your heart from the earliest days of your life.

I am also impressed with the transparency of this book. Richie takes us through some of the very personal and private moments of his own life. Events that could have derailed his dream all become part of the story of how important it is to push through and win. I believe as you take this journey with him, your life will be changed for the better. As you read, open your heart and discover the God-designed dream deep inside that is waiting to be released.

Thanks, Richie, for pushing through and writing this book. You living your dream will allow many to live theirs.

Chapter 1

CALLING ALL DREAMERS!

Dreams. Everyone has them. Understand, I'm not talking about nocturnal experiences or adventures that take place in your inner subconscious while in REM sleep! No, the dreams I'm referring to—your life-dreams—are much larger and carry far more significance. Even though they carry many different titles—your "life mission," your "God-given purpose and destiny," your "ultimate achievement in life," etc.—they all have the same end in mind. These are your life-dreams; and whether you believe it or not, *whether you feel like it or not*, you have one. Everyone does, and it begins in the earliest, formative years of life.

If you don't believe me, just spend a few hours in an elementary school lunchroom and ask the age-old question, "So, what do you want to be when you grow up?"

Talk about a dream fest!

Kids are quick to tell you their life-dream — at least, as they know it for their age. Little boys jump up and say, "I want to be a fireman when I grow up!" You also will hear answers like: an astronaut, a doctor, a policeman, or a professional athlete. Little girls aren't shy, either. Their dreams usually consist of becoming a teacher, a nurse, an actress, a singer, or even a veterinarian. Although the answers may greatly vary, one thing is consistent — everybody, at one time or another, has a dream.

Equaled with the joy of hearing young children scream out their desires is the sadness of listening to someone later in years who once had a dream but somewhere along the road lost their focus. Oftentimes, extreme disappointments and disillusions created by an apparent failure has halted their pursuit. Some grow too weary in the fight, while others are so mocked by their attempts and setbacks that they run in the opposite direction. Whatever the case may be, watching people — good, talented, educated, and ethical people — simply walk away from their dream is heart-wrenching.

That's exactly why I wrote this book.

LIVING THE DREAM

The world has always been full of dreamers. In the very first book of the Bible, Genesis, a young man named Joseph was called "the dreamer,"[1] but he wasn't alone.

Christopher Columbus dreamed of finding a new world where religious freedoms could be exercised. Michelangelo dreamed of a world filled with spectacular art. Beethoven dreamed of music being a prominent force in the earth. William Shakespeare dreamed of a world filled with literature. Thomas Edison's many dreams changed the face of the world as we know it. Martin Luther King, Jr. had a dream of racial equality. Bill Gates dreamed of the world working smarter and more efficiently through computers . . . and the list goes on and on. Today, our modern society has been fashioned by those who dared to dream . . . and actually did something about it.

To live your dream is the most fulfilling place you'll ever be. Notice, I didn't say it was the easiest! Living your dream, while ultra-satisfying, can be the hardest place on earth; but the *gain* far outweighs the *pain*. You just have to make up your mind that no matter what comes your way, you will never sell your dream to the lowest bidder. It may be tough — even seemingly unbearable, at times — but never turn loose of what God has placed inside your

> You just have to make up your mind that no matter what comes your way, you will never sell your dream to the lowest bidder.

heart. It's what you were put on this earth to do.

Everyone has a God-given dream (yes, including you), but the question is: How do you make it a reality? While there's not a one-size-fits-all answer, I do believe four-time Olympic gold medalist, Jesse Owens, has a great philosophy. He said it like this:

> "We all have dreams; but in order to make dreams come into reality, it takes an awful lot of determination, dedication, self-discipline, and effort."

In short, to live your dream, you have to DO something about it. You have to take action and start moving towards your dream right now, one step at a time. When you do, here are a few things to consider:

- **Dreams never come free**. There's a price tag attached to every dream. Think about it. If the dream came free, everybody would be living it! The truth is, dreams never come without a cost and sacrifice. For example, fulfilling your life's mission may require going back to school or burning the candle at both ends for a certain amount of time. You may have to pay a high price of social and economic status to follow your passion. Dr. Martin Luther King, Jr.'s dream cost him his very life. No matter how you slice it, dreams never come free.

A few years ago, I told our congregation how I would love to have a five-star restaurant in our church one day. The moment I said that, a young lady in our church knew this was to be part of her dream, as well. Instead of sitting around waiting for the right moment to happen, she did something about it—she went to culinary school! After graduating, she came right back to me and said, "Pastor Richie, are you still wanting that five-star restaurant here in the church?" I looked straight at her and without a blink I said, "Yes, Ma'am, we'll have it one day." She immediately replied, "Well, I just wanted to let you know that you're looking at your chef right here!" She made the sacrifice to position herself for her dream to come to pass.

Whether it's higher education, a specific certification, coaching in areas where you need help, or a change in lifestyle, there's a price tag to pay for your dream.

Be prepared to pay it.

- **Dreams come through a process**. Very rarely have I ever met anyone who loves the process of life! High school football players live for the Friday night lights, but they hate six a.m. workouts every Monday morning and the weight room training on Tuesday afternoons. They love the satisfaction of playing the game, but the process to prepare is a completely different story. Your life-dream is much the same way. It will not happen overnight; it's a process.

One of my spiritual mentors, Pastor Mike Hayes, whom I'll be quoting throughout this book, once said a statement that's helped me understand the value of process. He said:

> "Always be cautious of the 'fastest-growing' anything!"

What a powerful statement! The reason is quite simple: Usually, the "fastest-growing" something will one day be the "fastest-declining" something. Great things take time to develop. A grape doesn't become fine wine overnight, neither does a caterpillar turn into a beautiful butterfly in a day. It takes time; but in the end, the product is well worth the wait.

Something to always remember is this: The larger your dream, the longer the process. A mosquito is born within twenty-four hours of conception and only weighs about one milligram, but a female elephant can take up to two years before giving birth to babies that weigh over 200 pounds! If it seems like it's taking a long time for your dream to develop, don't be discouraged. It could be a sign that it's larger than you originally thought.

Your first move in the process might be finding the courage to leave your comfort zone. Most of the time, you can't stay where you are and reach your ultimate destination in life. Anyone who's ever lived out their life-dream has endured the discomfort of launching out into the unknown. You will, too. Don't be afraid, just embrace the process.

- **Dreams always have obstacles to overcome.** I once heard a man say that if you tell your dream to people and they don't look at you like you're crazy, you're probably dreaming too small! Some people will be your cheer-leaders, some won't understand at all, while others will be haters and try everything in their power to crush your spirit. Whatever the case may be, get ready for resistance, especially the "You can't do that. That's impossible!" response

> Most of the time, you can't stay where you are and reach your ultimate destination in life.

from people. When you hear this—and you will—know this one thing: People accomplish the so-called "impossible" all the time. Now, it's your turn.

It's time to overcome the obstacles and change history.

Chuck Yeager began his military career as an aircraft mechanic in the United States Army, but there was much more on the inside of him. In time, he became the first person in history to break the sound barrier, but not without overcoming great opposition.

Before his world record flight, several other pilots had attempted this same mission, but all failed. They reported that at certain speeds the aircraft shook so violently, it felt like the entire plane was about to disintegrate. Their results were all the same: Fear conquered, the opposition won, and the sound barrier was never broken. That was until Captain Yeager decided to live his dream, despite the obstacles and other people's failures.

On October 14, 1947, two days after he was thrown from a horse and suffered two broken ribs, Army fighter pilot Capitan Chuck Yeager did what no one dreamed possible. He took a Bell-X1 rocket jet up to 45,000 feet and flew over 700 miles per hour, breaking the sound barrier with a sonic boom. He experienced the same difficulties and fears in the cockpit as all the other pilots who tried and failed. What was the difference? Chuck Yeager pressed through the discomfort, fear, and pain to reach his dream and change history. He did what everyone else didn't do — overcame the obstacles.

Never let opposition, people's negative opinions, or circumstances stop your dream. At times, you'll be forced to navigate through dry, lonely, and unproductive seasons of life. Other times, it may seem as though you're going backwards instead of forwards. In those moments, let me assure you that what seems to be a *setback* can turn into a *setup* for something greater.

Decide now to push through opposition.

- **Help others establish their dream first.** World-renowned motivational speaker, Zig Ziglar, established this principle best, when he said:

> "You can have everything in life you want, if you will just help enough other people get what they want."

My wife, Leann, and I have lived this motto for years. The outcome? It's simple. The more we help people find, prepare, launch, and fulfill their dream, the more we find ourselves living in the middle of ours! I can tell you, there's nothing better.

The Bible records the story of two men — neither who were satisfied with the status quo of life — Elijah and Elisha. Elijah was an older, wiser man whom God had called to be a prophet to the nations. The biblical recording of his life is nothing short of supernatural, but it was nothing compared to what happened to his understudy, Elisha.

One day, these two men were walking and Elijah asked Elisha, "What can I do for you?" In other words, he asked, "Elisha, what's your dream? How can I help make it come to pass?" Immediately, Elisha answered, "Let me have a double portion of your spirit." Just then, Elijah was taken up to Heaven and Elisha received exactly what he requested.[2]

Wouldn't you have loved to have been Elisha that day — to tell someone your dream and have it immediately dropped in your lap? Sure you would! (Even better to be Elijah — the one who made Elisha's dream come true.) But, there's a bit more to this story.

You see, Elisha just didn't show up that day out of the blue. It was quite the opposite. Before this amazing encounter, Elisha had been serving Elijah for six years. During that time, Elisha did everything he could to help Elijah live his dream. In the end, Elisha received a greater reward and walked in his ultimate calling for sixty years! Six for sixty is a pretty good trade off.

If you want to live out your life's purpose and divine destiny, then help someone live theirs, first. The Bible is true; you will reap what you sow[3]—sometimes double!

FIRSTHAND KNOWLEDGE

Contrary to what you may have heard from others, it is possible to passionately pursue, live, and achieve your dream, mission, purpose, and destiny to the highest level. Will it come easy? Surely not. Dreams are never accomplished without a fight! The reason is simple. Not only do you have a God-given mission innately deposited within your DNA, you also have an enemy whose sole purpose is to steal, kill, and destroy that dream no matter what it takes—and your enemy is a master at his job![4] There will be battles on

> Dreams are never accomplished without a fight!

every front, but the good news is there's a greater power on the inside of you than the ones that come against you.[5] You have to rely on and fully trust the "Greater One" — the One who gave you the dream to begin with — to equip you with strength, direction, wisdom, and courage. He's well able.

I can testify, firsthand.

My family and I have made it thus far on our journey primarily due to two things: God's grace and the application of His Word in our lives. To look back at what we've had to endure and conquer is nothing short of miraculous. Many of these stories and experiences are spread throughout the pages of this book.

Let me make one thing perfectly clear. I don't know it all (There's only One who does!); and I don't claim to be an expert on "How to make your dreams come true." All I can attest to is what we've had to walk through and the principles which have guided us all along the way. They work because of one simple fact: The Word of God works.

If you're in any form of leadership position, whether you're the pastor of a church (like me), the CEO of an organization getting off the ground, or a college student pressing through the drudge of classes towards your degree, the pressure to throw in the towel and walk away from your dream is enormous. I know; I've been there, oh, so many times! But, I also can say that no matter how hard it seems, there's always a tomorrow and there's strength for you during dark times of doubt, discouragement, disillusionment, and despair. If you've experienced times like these and you're looking for encouragement to keep walking through the tests and trials, then you've picked up the right book!

HEAR THE CALL

If you're twenty years old or eighty years old, I'm calling all dreamers! Calling all dreamers to man their post, revive their courage, strengthen their resolve, and live their dream. YOLO is an acronym for "You Only Live Once." Even though it's a modern-day slang term for teens, it's the truth nonetheless! You *do* only live once, so you might as well live your dream and fulfill the calling on the inside of you. If you don't, then who will?

No one.

Popular American author and motivational speaker, Les Brown, said it best:

"The graveyard is the richest place on earth, because it is here that you will find all the hopes and dreams that were never fulfilled, the books that were never written, the songs that were never sung, the inventions that were never shared, the cures that were never discovered, all because someone was too afraid to take that first step, keep with the problem, or determined to carry out their dream."

You're never too young or too old to dream. Don't let your life go by and not fulfill what God has placed in you to accomplish. That would be tragic. Rise above your past failures and/or the paralyzing fear of the future that's keeping you from moving full steam ahead towards your passions. It's time to dream.

Calling all dreamers! The world is your canvas. Let your passion be your brush strokes. Make the decision to move towards what God has orchestrated for you to achieve without hesitation or fear, laying aside everything that so easily distracts you. Are you ready? I know you are.

Let the dreams begin.

Chapter 2

TWO SIMPLE WORDS

Fifty.
  Sixty-six.
Forty-one.
Sixty.
Fifty-four.
If you're a sports nut like me, you're probably waiting for, "Hut . . . hut," next! Sadly, these numbers aren't part of a football snap cadence. Instead, they represent real facts about real people.

- Fifty: the percentage of new businesses that fail within their first five years of operation.[1]
- Sixty-six: the percentage of businesses that fail after ten years or more.[2]
- Forty-one: the percentage of first marriages that end in divorce.[3]
- Sixty: the percentage of failed second marriages.[4]

- Fifty-four: the percentage of college students who enter college but never graduate.[5]

Add to this number the 4,000 churches that close their doors for the last time each year and the 1,500 pastors who quit the ministry *each month* in the United States alone.[6] We have an epidemic on our hands . . .

. . . The epidemic of quitting.

There have been countless numbers of times I've had to face the battle of giving up and walking away from my unfulfilled and unfinished dream, but what was instilled in me at a young age has kept me from falling prey to that temptation. It came from the hero of my life, Donald (Donnie) Ralph Mullis.

My dad.

"ONE THING WE NEVER DO"

Time will only record how many things Dad said that have shaped my life over the years and continue to do so to this day. Actually, the principles he and my mother imparted into me are now defining my children, their grandchildren. I will be eternally grateful for their influence, prayer, support, and love no matter what I did or how crazy I acted during certain seasons of life.

Of all the things Dad told me, one of the most important statements came when I was very young; and it has rang in my ears thousands of times. I can still hear his powerful, southern Georgia draw as he engraved these words on my young, impressionable heart:

"Richie, you're a Mullis, and one thing we never do — we never, ever quit. Do you understand that? We don't quit!"

My dad was the best at making me feel like I could achieve anything I wanted, and he made sure that quitting was never on my radar! When I wanted to play football or baseball, he reminded me of his rules before I ever signed up. "Richie," he would bark, "If you want to play, that's fine; but understand this, you're not quitting until the season is over — win or lose, good team or bad team, or whether if you play or ride the bench. Understand?" "Yes sir! I'm not quitting!"

It was never an option.

Until . . .

MY FIRST CHANCE

The year was 1983. The place was Snellville, Georgia. I was nine years old and was playing baseball for the South Gwinnett Athletic Association's Cardinals. Yes, it was only Little League, but to me, I was living my dream and this was my first stop on the way to play for my favorite team, the Atlanta Braves. (They're still my favorite to this day!) There was only one problem: I was the worst player on a really bad team!

Being the kid with the least amount of talent on any team isn't fun; but when the whole team is bad and you're still the worst player, that's even worse. No matter how faithful I was to practice, it never seemed to help. Thus, I sat the bench every single game. If I ever did get to play (probably because the coach felt sorry for me), I played the position where I could cause the least amount of damage—right field. It was a season I'll never forget mostly because how embarrassing it was to lose every game so badly.

Watching our games was gruesome, but my dad was faithful to come out and support. One day after we had experienced another humiliating defeat, we were driving home and I cried all the way. Out of nowhere, Dad leaned over and said the words I never imagined he would say. "Richie, I know you're really having a hard time this year, and it's obvious you're miserable. If you want to quit, you can." What??? A Mullis quitting on something? Are you kidding me? This was unheard of! It was like an alien who looked just like my father came and took over his body for a minute! For the very first time I can ever remember, the choice to quit was staring me right in the face. Now, it was up to me. What would I do? Would I take the easy road or stay true to our Mullis creed? The temptation was so inviting, but I knew what my dad had drilled into me over and over again, so I made my decision.

I didn't quit!

As much as I hated that season, I found out a fact about my life: Something *in me* was bigger than the circumstances that *surrounded me*. In hindsight, I've often wondered if my dad was really serious or just testing me. Whatever the case, I stuck it out until the end of the season. The fact that I stayed didn't make the team any better, but it birthed something in me: the will to stay with things in the worst of situations. Only God knew how many times I would face that same option throughout my life. And, in every situation, no matter how much I wanted to abandon my dream, my resolve has been the same as when I was at nine years old.

We don't quit!

A DIFFERENT PLAN

Growing up was tough for me. One of my most pivotal years was the seventh grade, mainly because I was a short, overweight kid who ate lunch by himself every day. I really had no friends, so the only way I knew to gain attention was through fighting. It became such my way of life that I was once suspended from school for being in two fights . . . in the same day! When my dad came to pick me up, we didn't go home;

> Something *in me* was bigger than the circumstances that *surrounded me*.

instead, we drove straight to a health club. On the way, Dad said, "Richie, if you're going to fight, then you need to learn to win!"

A journey began that day that would reshape my physical life.

From that time all the way through high school, I committed to training in the gym several days a week. By the time I graduated, I had entered the Mr. Teen Atlanta body building competition and took fourth place in my division. My dream, after high school, was to walk on and play football for the University of West Georgia. I had the physical skillset, all I needed was a chance.

But, God had a different plan.

WHEN I FACE A MOUNTAIN

My family was always involved in church throughout my entire life. One Sunday morning, after being out drinking with my friends the entire night before, I came to church and my Mom recognized something was wrong. After that service, she and dad dropped a bomb-shell on me. They said, "Richie, this is it. You're done. You're moving out." At first, that was music to my ears as I was ready to head to Carrolton, Georgia to chase my dream of playing football, but that's not quite what they had in mind!

"We know you want to go to UWG, but the only school we're going to pay for is Lee University!"

My immediate reaction was, "Are you kidding me? A Bible college with a bunch of nerds and Bible-thumpin' Christian youth group kids? NO WAY!"

But, they won.

Once I landed at Lee University in Cleveland, Tennessee, my mind was set on joining a fraternity for the simple reason of having a place to belong. While being in the fraternity was an answer to my quest, something much more significant awaited me: the frat motto. At the time, it seemed senseless and stupid, but little did I know how it would become a foundational truth for my life's journey. The motto, which I still have memorized to this day, is this:

"When I face a mountain, I will not quit. I will try to climb over it, find a way around it, or tunnel underneath. Or, perhaps stay just where I am and turn it into a gold mine with God's helping hand."

Talk about divine providence! God surely knew how many opportunities to quit would present themselves to me over the years and how much I would rely on this motto for my life.

It's been a life-saver countless numbers of times.

A COMPLETE LIFE CHANGE

I really only had two ambitions my first two years in college. (Sadly, serving God wasn't one of them!) They were to play baseball and meet girls. I was living the so-called college dream. Then, everything changed.

The summer between my sophomore and junior year, I was invited to serve as a life guard at a youth camp in Florida. On the second night of camp, July 2, 1996, God rocked my world! All of my life, I'd been in church, heard hundreds of sermons, and now I was even attending a Bible college; yet, I still had never fully surrendered my life to Jesus. That night, it all changed! I can't even begin to articulate everything that happened, except to say I went into that service one way and came out a completely changed young man. God had done a work in me that practically no one could believe, especially those who knew me well. But, it was for real.

Not only did I meet Jesus in a real way that summer, but I also met a man who became very influential in my life, a youth evangelist named Chuck Ramsey. He was the coolest Christian—not to mention the coolest preacher—I'd ever seen or heard. He made such an impact on me that I decided to put school on pause that fall and travel with him full-time. It would prove to be one of the best decisions I've ever made.

Usually, when people travel with someone like Chuck, they have some type of musical talent. Notice, I said, "Usually!" This wasn't the case for me. Having practically zero musical talent, my job was to simply drive from town to town and set up whatever was needed for the meetings. Basically, I was a roadie. Many times after we finished a meeting or camp, I would break everything down, load it up, and then drive all night just to arrive at the next engagement to unload and set it all up once again. There was nothing pretty or exciting about this job, but it didn't matter to me. I was doing exactly what God wanted me to do.

After a few months of consistent travel — one town to the next every week — I was restless and began questioning my next step. My options were to stay on the road with Chuck, go back to Lee University, or join a church staff as a youth pastor. I went to Chuck to seek his advice and his answer was far more impacting than he could've ever imagined. He said, "Richie, the truth is, you have great abilities and can do a bunch of different things. But, there's something about finishing what you've started that will not only speak on your resume, but will also help you in the future when you feel like quitting!"

When I heard these words, a phrase that I had known for years popped into my head as a confirmation of what Chuck was saying:

"The greatest ability you can ever have is
stick-ability."

> "The greatest ability you can ever have is stick-ability."

Once I heard his words, I knew exactly what I was to do: return to Lee University and finish my degree. I really didn't make that commitment for anyone but me. During my last years of college, Chuck's words rolled over and over in my mind and spirit. So many times my stick-ability was tested; but in the end, I conquered. Not only did I finish my degree, I also met the one person who could actually see real potential in me . . .

. . . My wife, Leann.

Leann saw my potential, but her friends . . . well, that was a different story. They only remembered the old Richie—the person I was before my camp experience with Jesus. Somewhere in the back of their minds, they knew Leann could do better, so they did everything possible to talk her out of dating me. Thankfully, she didn't listen to them! Instead, she went against all of their advice and chose to believe in me—or rather, the gift of God *in* me. Thank God she did!

After one year of dating and a five-month engagement, Leann and I were married. (I guess we proved all her friends wrong!) I had one semester to finish before graduation and after that, we immediately took off into full-time ministry and have never looked back.

NEVER, EVER, EVER

Not only did my father and Chuck Ramsey instill the will to never quit into me, there was one other person who God used to make sure I got the message—Pastor Mitch Maloney.

Pastor Maloney was a huge part of my spiritual development while in college. It always amazed me how he really didn't have any idea who I was, but many times would point me out and ask me to lunch. This man, who was the pastor of thousands, believed in me and invested the time to pour into my life. I'm so grateful till this day.

One day while at lunch, Pastor Maloney told me, "Richie, there was a time in my ministry where I wanted to quit so badly, that I actually was going to drive to our state's denominational office and hand in my resignation." He continued, "I had made up my mind that I was quitting; but just as I got into my car, I put in a (cassette) tape and the very first thing I heard was, 'I have a word for someone today who feels like giving up: STAY!' I knew God was speaking to me, so I turned around, went back to my office, and shredded my letter."

Being a college kid who only saw what everyone else saw—a great man with a large, thriving church, a great family, and one who was taking the time to mentor me—I couldn't fathom why he would resign. It looked like he had the world by the tail; but not everything is as it seems from the outside. I've come to learn that even the ones who have it "all together" face the temptation to walk away, too.

He concluded our lunch by saying, "Richie, there's going to come a time when you will want to quit and give up. I'm here to tell you, quitting is never an option. Never, ever, ever, ever give up!"

There have been many people who, over my lifetime, have spoken powerful statements and words of encouragement to me; but hardly any compare to the weightiness and effectiveness which were uttered by Pastor Maloney that day. Today, I'm a testimony that his advice works, and it will work for you, too.

No matter where you are in the process of living your dream, embracing two simple words can become your foundation to success: NEVER QUIT! Legendary coach, Vince Lombardi said it this way:

"Winners never quit and quitters never win."

Such a true statement. There's been too much invested in you to quit. Commit to follow the example of Jesus who is the author AND finisher of your faith.[7] The Bible says that He who began a good work in you will bring it to completion.[8] Jesus is not only a starter, but a finisher — and you are, as well.

It's easy to start, but it takes a real champion to finish. I like to say it like this:

Remember the guy who gave up?
No one else does either.

My testimony is probably very similar to anyone who's been living and building their dream for any length of time: If I had a dollar for every time I wanted to quit, I'd be a millionaire! Yes, the opportunities to walk away have been numerous and to stick it out has oftentimes been costly; but anything of value always costs something. You must make up your mind — *even before you begin to walk out your dream* — that quitting is not an option.

> . . . anything of value always cost something.

The formula to success is this: Dream big. Stay the course. Finish strong. Never quit. It's simply not an option.

Even in the most difficult of times.

Chapter 3

PRESS ON!

To list all the incidents, where the enormous pressure to quit was staring Leann and I in the face, but we didn't, is another book on its own. However, never have we faced so much pressure as when we made the decision to start our own church. To say that all hell broke loose on us would be the understatement of the year! We didn't know much about church planting, but one thing we learned very quickly was this: If we could make it through this, we can make it through ANYTHING!

Thank God, we have.

STARTING OUT

After serving several years as youth pastors for some great churches, Leann and I knew God had something more for us. A larger dream was stirring on the inside of our hearts and it was time to act. While on staff at a church in East Texas, we began to prepare our exit and look for a place close to the Dallas metro area to plant a church. We knew the timing was right, so we were obedient to scout out the land.

For a few weeks, we drove to the Dallas area every weekend looking for the place God wanted us to be. On practically every trip, we stopped at a Dairy Queen® in this little country town called Forney, Texas. Neither of us had ever heard of this town—and we were sure no one else had, either—but that was all about to change.

One day while driving around looking for prospective places to hold services, our real estate agent asked me, "Have you guys ever considered Forney?" I looked at her like she had lost her mind. I knew planting the church in this location would be a real stretch for Leann, so I called her from the car to get her opinion.

> *"Baby, I'm out with the realtor right now. What do you think about looking for property in Forney?"*
>
> *"Where's that?"*
>
> *"You know, it's the town where we stop at Dairy Queen® all the time."*
>
> *"Richie, are you kidding me? That's in the middle of nowhere!"*

Obviously, it wasn't our first choice of locations, but we were open to anything God had for us. So, we looked and this is what we discovered: God was about to turn this little town into much more than a stop for gasoline and hamburgers.

It was the exact place He had designed for us to plant the church.

In the fall of 2004, we started Sunday evening Bible studies. Mind you, no one knew us or knew anything about us. We weren't a "plant" from another church with financial backing and a core team of families who were moving to help us. We were completely on our own. However, we figured there would be at least four people (two friends and two family members) who would join to help us, but none of them came—not even our family members! No, sir. It was me, Leann, and our daughters. That was the church! It was the most nerve-racking time of our lives, but we knew we were following God's plan.

After six weeks, the Bible study grew to twenty-three people—our family of five and eighteen others. In November, we all met at a barbeque restaurant where I announced that there would be no meetings throughout the holidays; but in January, we would be back in full swing. Those six weeks of waiting, during which we resigned our position at the church in East Texas, sold our house, and packed up everything we owned, seemed like an eternity.

January came rolling around, and we were off to the big metropolis of Forney, Texas. Sadly, this is what

The pressure to abort our dream hammered my mind every day.

greeted us: Of the eighteen additional people we gained in the fall, *only one family came back in January!* That's right. Only one. We were right back where we started . . . with our five plus one family.

Before we could even get all of our boxes unpacked, I was already thinking, *Richie, what in the world have you done? You've moved your family out here to the middle of nowhere, and you only have one other family in the church! Have you lost your mind?*

One of the main reasons I questioned our decision was during those six weeks of transition, we were offered youth pastor positions from large churches, all with very appealing financial packages! Oh, yeah, I was questioning our every move at this point. The pressure to abort our dream hammered my mind every day. But, one thing kept me grounded: the dream inside.

We had to press on.

With no permanent place to meet, we held Friday night Bible Studies in an elementary school. Within a week or so, three more people started to attend, then four, then five, but this was moving way to slow for me. So, I did the only thing I knew to do: I took the Forney phone book and started making calls, beginning with the A's! My job during the day was to call every single person in Forney and tell them we were starting a church. Much to my surprise, IT WORKED! The next Friday, three new families came to our Bible study.

I thought I had won the lottery!

Our official church launch came on Easter 2005, three months after we had relocated. On that day, fifty-seven people came. We thought we had a mega-church on our hands! Of course, some were friends who wanted to support (and some who just flat out felt sorry for us), but it didn't matter. It was a record crowd, and I was on top of the world . . . until the following few weeks.

The next week, our attendance was thirty-nine. The next week, twenty-seven. Nineteen came through the door the following week and then seventeen the next. We finally leveled out around twenty people for the next two months, which seemed like five years to me. Something had to change, so we produced a door hanger and canvased neighborhoods. The next Sunday, nine new families showed up—and seven stayed! Thankfully, we were finally seeing some progress, . . . and then it happened. The opportunities to throw our hands up and walk away came in like a flood!

WHEN IT RAINS . . .

After five months of hard work, labor, toil, sweat, and basically breaking our backs to do everything possible to help grow the church, we were averaging fifty people in attendance. Throughout my life, I've built very successful businesses from the ground up; trained, competed, and placed in national bodybuilding competitions; and grew youth ministries from practically zero to thousands of students in attendance, but nothing—absolutely nothing—had ever been as exhausting and taxing on me as this was. It was time for a talk with God.

One day while driving and praying in my truck—something I do a lot—I told the Lord, "God, we've given You everything and things seem to be getting worse instead of better." Just then, I heard the Lord say, "No, Richie, you haven't given me everything. You have $6,000 in your bank account right now." I knew God was leading us to empty our account and give that amount into the Kingdom, so we did. I also knew that according to Malachi 3:10, the windows of Heaven were about to open in response to our giving. Well, some windows opened alright, but they weren't the windows of Heaven! Just the opposite.

All hell broke loose.

THE BITE

Right after we emptied our bank account, I was out seeing some people in a neighboring town about fifteen minutes away from our house. My phone rang and I could see it was Leann, so I excused myself from my conversation and took the call. I could've never imagined what I was about to hear. On the other end of the phone, my wife was hysterical.

> *"Richie! Richie!"*
> *"What, babe? What's wrong? Is everything ok?"*
> *"Richie, you've got to get home now! The girls and I were in the backyard and Ashtyn* (our middle daughter) *was just bitten by a snake!"*
> *"What? Are you kidding me? What kind of snake?"*
> *"I don't know! She screamed and it crawled off!"*
> *"Call 9-1-1. I'm on the way!"*

You can only imagine the thoughts that raced through my mind. I drove as fast as I could to get home to my family. When the ambulance arrived, they immediately took Ashtyn to Children's Hospital in Dallas where the E.R. doctors were very concerned. Before they could give her any anti-venom, they had to know what kind of snake bit her. Not knowing this information could make the treatment more lethal than the bite. We had no idea what to tell them. All we knew to do was to pray.

The medical staff kept very close tabs on her for the next few hours. After we had prayed, they finally released her with no side effects! While we were so thankful that God had touched her body, my mind was consumed with the thoughts of *You know, Richie, if you hadn't have moved out here, this would've never happened.*

But, this was just the beginning.

THE BOTCH

About two weeks later, I was on a ministry trip in Georgia and Leann was back home in Texas. Throughout her life, Leann has always suffered with migraine headaches, but this night the pain was exceptional; so much so that her mom called the ambulance, and they took Leann to the emergency room. On the way to the hospital, her mom called me in a panic. Of course, me being over 1,000 miles away didn't help matters either.

Leann and her mom's concern stemmed from a recent experience with Leann's sister. The day after giving birth to her baby, she suffered a seizure, a stroke, and a heart attack. Knowing that bleeding on the brain was in Leann's genes, they wanted to take every precaution available. Once at the hospital, the doctors did a spinal tap and the results were good. All was well with my wife; however, not all was well with the procedure.

> The hole from the spinal tap was not plugged correctly, and Leann had been losing fluid off her brain.

Instead of her getting better, Leann's headaches worsened day after day; until we finally were forced to go back to the hospital. The doctors did another exam and found what we never expected: The hole from the spinal tap was not plugged correctly, and Leann had been losing fluid off her brain. Not only was Leann in horrible pain 24/7, but she could experience permanent brain damage if it wasn't immediately corrected. The situation was grim, so the doctors scheduled an emergency surgery. Again, we needed God's healing hand at work.

Thankfully, the surgery was a success; but the emotional trauma—especially on the heels of our daughter's experience—was tough. Was God trying to tell us something? Had we really made the right move? Was it time to pack up, lick our wounds, count our losses, and move on? These were just a few of the questions we had to face. However, every time a question or doubt would pop up, I would remember the dream inside of my heart and knew that we must keep pressing on.

THE BURN

As if this wasn't enough, we encountered another incident only a few weeks later. One afternoon, I was in our home talking to a friend on the phone when I heard Leann yelling something. I couldn't understand one word she said, so I told my friend I would call him back. Leaving the room, I met Leann in the hallway, and I quickly saw the reason for her panic: *Our kitchen was on fire!*

Again, another 9-1-1 call. (We should've put it on speed dial! Again, another traumatic experience; and again, another intervention by God. The firemen arrived at our house in almost record time and were able to put out the blaze before it consumed anything but the kitchen.

Just like the previous events, God worked on our behalf, but the emotional drain was about to get the best of us.

THE BOTTOM

The day after the fire, we decided to meet Leann's parents in Dallas for lunch. Believe me, we needed a break! We thought it would be a nice getaway day, but as soon as I started the car the "check engine" light came on. Thankfully, Leann's dad was a mechanic, so I just figured he could check it out once we were there. No problem, right? Well, it wasn't an issue until we were on our way . . . in the middle of the freeway . . . in the middle of traffic . . . when all of the sudden – "Bam!" One of our tires blew out! This only added more fuel to our emotional fire.

Here we were, stuck on the side of the highway, when Leann's mom and dad came to our rescue. They drove separate cars, so the girls jumped in with Leann's mom while I went and sat in the truck with my father-in-law. As soon as I sat down, it happened.

The meltdown began.

I started to cry and my father-in-law, not knowing all that was going on in me, put his hand on my back and said, "Hey, don't be so upset. It's just a flat tire! No big deal. We got this." I looked at him and said, "Cecil, it's not the tire. I'm running on fumes!" And, at that point, even the fumes were about to run out.

But, the dream was still alive.

TIE A KNOT AND HANG ON

By now, we were all questioning. *God, what's going on here? Here we were working day and night, pastoring and loving our people, raising our family, emptying our bank account, doing everything we know to do, and yet all of this turmoil. What are you trying to say?*

As the leader of our home and church, I was bombarded with doubts seemingly every minute of the day. My daughter had been bitten by a snake, my wife rushed to surgery, our kitchen on fire, and now car trouble. Had I completely blown it? Was leading my family out here something birthed of my own desire and not God's? Why was all of this happening? Frankly, I was at the end of my rope! It was then I remembered President Franklin D. Roosevelt's famous words:

No matter how difficult or how many obstacles you face on the road to your dream, don't stop pursuing it.

"When you reach the end of your rope, tie a
knot in it and hang on!"

Believe me, I was hanging on to the knot.

No matter how difficult or how many obstacles you
face on the road to your dream, don't stop pursuing it.
When you're faced with times of discouragement,
remember these words from the Apostle Paul:

*". . . But one thing I do: Forgetting what is behind
and straining toward what is ahead, I press on
toward the goal to win the prize for which God
has called me heavenward in Christ Jesus."*

Philippians 3:13-14 (NIV)

Two of the most important things from these powerful
scriptures are:

1. Forgetting what's behind. The past is the past.
   You can't do anything to change it. Pick up
   from here and learn from past mistakes/
   victories. It's time to live your dream, today.
2. Pressing on to what God has called you to do.
   Move forward. Make progress. Don't stop until
   you have obtained the prize. This is your time.

World-renown author, Napoleon Hill, once said:

"Patience, persistence and perspiration
make an unbeatable combination for success."

Your dream is alive! Be patient. Keep working towards what God has called you to do. Forget the past. And, in spite of every attack to set you back, press on!

You'll be glad you did.

Chapter 4

THE MIRACLE OF EMPTINESS

Looking at the title of this chapter, you might think it's a misprint! Very rarely, if ever, are the words "miracle" and "emptiness" used in the same phrase, as they appear contradictory to each other; but I assure you, it's not a typo. They *do* go together beautifully. There is, in fact, a miracle of emptiness; and when you activate it in your life, the windows of Heaven open up!

Throughout this chapter, we will be referring to a very familiar passage of scripture found in 2 Kings 4. Now, before you get to the first verse and say, "Oh, I've read this before," let me encourage you to read it all the way through. Then, let the Lord begin to reveal a new view of this story to you. With that in mind, let's look at the story of Elisha and his encounter with a woman — a pastor's wife, if you will — who has lost her husband and is about to lose her sons, as well.

"The wife of a man from the company of the prophets cried out to Elisha, 'Your servant my husband is dead, and you know that he revered the LORD. *But now his creditor is coming to take my two boys as his slaves.' Elisha replied to her, 'How can I help you? Tell me, what do you have in your house?' 'Your servant has nothing there at all,' she said, 'except a small jar of olive oil.' Elisha said, 'Go around and ask all your neighbors for empty jars. Don't ask for just a few. Then go inside and shut the door behind you and your sons. Pour oil into all the jars, and as each is filled, put it to one side.' She left him and shut the door behind her and her sons. They brought the jars to her and she kept pouring. When all the jars were full, she said to her son, 'Bring me another one.' But he replied, 'There is not a jar left.' Then the oil stopped flowing. She went and told the man of God, and he said, 'Go, sell the oil and pay your debts. You and your sons can live on what is left.' "*

2 Kings 4:1-7 (NIV)

Welcome to the "miracle of emptiness!"

EMPTY FROM THE START

Leann and I know a thing or two about being empty. As a matter of fact, our church was literally built on emptiness.

We moved to Forney on two things: A dream in our hearts and faith. That's it. I've known people who have stepped out, like us, to start a church, but with tons of money. (I'm not saying that having money is wrong. Lord knows we could've used it!) Some start with cash and pledges from governing bodies or sponsoring churches in excess of $100,000. Believe me, you can make some noise in a community with those kind of resources! But, Leann and I didn't have that type of funding. When we moved, we had $21,000 to our name. That was to raise a family of five PLUS buy all the things we needed for the church like a sound system, children's ministry equipment, fliers and advertising, and rent. No church sent us monthly "start up" support, nor did we receive any help from the denomination where we were raised. It was us and God.

Unlike most church plants, we didn't have a "plant team" to help us launch. We were it. We didn't have a set up and tear down team. We were it! There was no worship team or children's ministry workers. We were it! Every Sunday morning at seven a.m. sharp, come rain or shine, me, Leann, and our daughters drove to the elementary school where we rented their cafeteria/ auditorium to start setting up for the morning service. Many times, the only people who were *in* the service were the very same ones who helped set up! We were empty, but we were poised for God to something super- natural.

THREE LITTLE WORDS

When the church was just starting, I thought I had to have the answers for everything. After all, I am the leader, right? But, here's what I quickly found out: I don't have all the answers! Actually, I've been brought to the place where I realize how little I do know. It's an emptying of myself.

Over the years, I've come to embrace three little words more than any three words in the English language (with the exception of "I love you" to my beautiful wife and three daughters). They're the key to emptying of yourself and I believe that anyone who is moving into their God-given dream needs to have them imprinted on their mind and never far from their tongue! Those three little words are:

"I DON'T KNOW!"

You've probably never heard this taught at any church growth conferences or read it in the latest business-building book or blog; but if you want to position your-self for God to take you from where you are to another plateau, emptiness has to be a part of your fabric.

Several times throughout the years, our staff (or Leann) have looked at me and asked, "Pastor Richie, where's the money coming from to pay the bills this week?" That used to weigh heavy on me; but today, when asked such a question, I say with a confident smile, "I don't know!" People in our congregation ask me, "Pastor, when's my miracle going to happen?" I look them in the eye, smile, and say, "I don't know!"

When you start realizing that your dream isn't based on you and your wisdom, but rather on God and His unlimited wisdom, power, and resources; then it becomes very easy to let those three words roll off your tongue. your mouth. It's a sign that you're being emptied.

TOO MUCH

If you're in the process of building a church, a ministry, or a business, let me tell you something else you might not have never heard:

Some people are overqualified!

Let me explain this statement a bit further.

When the U.S. economy plummeted in 2008, many people lost their jobs. There were thousands of people, with a resume that would turn the head of any CEO, who couldn't find a job anywhere. People with multiple master's degrees had a hard time finding jobs as waiters/waitress at local restaurants. Why? Because they were overqualified for the position.

The job market isn't the only place where this prin-

Success comes because of emptiness, more than abilities.

ciple comes into play. It applies spiritually, as well. Sometimes, we simply have "too much" and need to be emptied.

When Elisha asked the widow, "What do you have?" I believe he wasn't asking to see if she had enough, but rather, did she have *too much?* Do you remember when God called Moses to lead the Children of Israel out of Egypt's bondage? One of the first things God asked Moses was, "What is that in your hand?" Moses answered, "A rod." Immediately, God said, "Cast it on the ground."[1]

Why did God say such a thing? Because Moses had too much. God said, "Release it!" and when Moses did, miracles began to happen.

Today, too many people are trying to build their God-given dream by their own strengths, talents, education, abilities, money, and gifts. Don't get me wrong; I'm a 100% believer in using everything God has given you to bring about His dream for your life. But, there comes a time when you have to step back and say, "There's just too much 'me' in this equation." When you get to this point, here's good news: You're about to experience the miracle of emptiness!

Let's take a look at a few areas where you can have

"too much."

Too much talent. In all my ministry life (which is practically my entire adult life), I've seen very few churches or organizations who didn't have enough talent to succeed. The problem isn't having a pool of talent; the problem many times is having *too much* talent. Believe me, as a church, it's so easy to fall into a false sense of security that says, "Our music team will build this church," or "Our great children's workers will make us grow." At the beginning, Leann and I fell into this trap, thinking that our success was going to rise or fall on our abilities and talents. Boy, were we completely wrong! What we've come to realize is this: Success comes because of *emptiness* more than *abilities*.

Yes, every organization needs talented people to succeed, but you can never rely solely on talents and leave out the Spirit of God! There are times where you must step aside and allow Him to do what only He can do.

Too much knowledge and strength. Not only can you put too much confidence in your own abilities, you can also credit far too much of your success on your own human knowledge and strength. Have you ever known someone who was about to lose it all and God was the only thing that could save them? Then, after He brought them out of the pit and their life turned around, they don't need God any longer! In their eyes, it was *their* tenacity, *their* strength, *their* dedication, or *their* education that brought them out of the mud. How easy it is, especially in times of prosperity, to look inward and believe that your success strictly came from your efforts. The truth is that success in any endeavor comes not by your might, nor by your power, but by the Spirit of the living God.[2] A life of emptiness always recognizes His working.

Too much agenda. Maybe having too much talent and/ or too much of your own knowledge and strength isn't your issue, but how about being over-dependent on your own agenda and plans? In other words, you organize God right out the back door of your life! I confess, I've always been one who likes to know every step of every day, but sometimes I have too much agenda. These are times when I have to put everything on hold, trash my plans for the day or week, and let God take over my schedule to do whatever He wants, whenever He wants, and however He wants to do it. It's amazing how much He can accomplish in a short amount of time.

Maybe you thought your dream was going to be a huge success totally based on your gifts, education, knowledge, and experience. Having those types of credentials can definitely help, but if you're looking for God—who is the master of making something out of nothing—to supernaturally bless your endeavors, then all of your natural qualifications, resources, and agenda must take a backseat. Like Moses, the "rod" in your hand might be too much!

Your "little" could be far more effective.

A LITTLE GOES A LONG WAY

The widow woman's admission of "I have nothing" wasn't the end of her statement. The next words out of her mouth were just as important: ". . . Except a small jar of olive oil." To many, this sounds like a statement of unbelief or, at best, small faith; but her "little" was all God needed.

Have you ever been in a season of life where you seemed to have little strength, little faith, little confidence in yourself, little joy, little vision, little hope, little money, etc.? If so, let me remind you of a song we used to sing in children's church that says, "Little is much when God is in it!" That's still the truth. When it seems that you only have a "little" bit of something, then you're in the perfect position for God's supernatural power to work a miracle for His glory!

Leann and I have been with "little" more times than I can count, but God has always provided. One year, we wanted to take our youth group to our denomination's annual youth conference. The deposit was only $100, but here was the problem: We only had fifty-seven cents in our youth account! I'd say that qualifies for "little," wouldn't you? Knowing how important this was to our youth, I asked our senior pastor if we could borrow the money from the church's general account, but that was a no go. We were in the perfect position for a miracle.

Five minutes after that conversation, a teenager walked into my office and slapped something down on my desk. I picked it up, and it was a check for $2,400 — from a kid! I said, "Man, where did you get this and why are you bringing it to me?" He said, "Pastor Richie, my dad (who didn't even attend church!) received a bonus at work, and he wanted to tithe it to our church!"

Who would've ever dreamed that a teenager would walk in and lay a check of that amount (or any amount for that matter!) on my desk? At the beginning of the day, we had little; but at the end, God made sure we had more than enough!

All throughout history, God's been changing some-one's "little" into something miraculous. Do you remember a young boy named David who lived in obscurity on the backside of a mountain? He was the little brother of all Jesse's sons. But, what did God do with this "little" boy? You know the story. David did something no other person in all of Israel could do — not the might-iest warrior, not the strongest of men, not the most valiant soldiers. He slayed the Philistine giant, Goliath; and that was just the beginning. In the end, David was the greatest king Israel had ever known. His military achievements are still unparalleled, and it all started when a "little" boy who used five "little" stones to do the miraculous.

In 1 Kings 18, Samaria had experienced a severe famine for three years. After hearing the Word of the Lord, the Prophet Elijah told his servant to go look for a sign of rain. Seven times he went, and on the seventh time he reported back to Elijah that there was a "little" cloud as small as a man's hand rising out of the sea.[3] That's all Elijah needed to hear! God was, once again, about to perform the miraculous out of what seemed to be sorely insufficient. The next verse says that the sky became black with *clouds*—plural. What started as something little changed into something amazing and ended the famine in the land.

In John 6, Jesus was on a hillside preaching and the crowd was growing hungry. After asking His disciples what was available to feed the multitude, a "little" boy with a "little" lunch came forward. It was barely enough to feed one person, not to mention the thousands who were in attendance that day, but then Jesus did something no one else could do: He took the "little" and made it more than enough!

How about Peter? Matthew 14 records one of the most well-known (and misquoted) stories of the New Testament—Peter's walk on the water. When Jesus came walking across the water towards the disciples' boat, they were all scared out of their minds. Peter begged the Lord to let him experience the same miracle, so Jesus told him to jump out. Peter obeyed and began to walk on the water, just like Jesus.

Now, this is where most people misinterpret the story. The minute Peter took his eyes off Jesus, he began to sink into the water. We've been taught that Peter sunk because he had *no faith*. That's not true! Look how Jesus described Peter's spiritual condition:

> *"Immediately Jesus reached out his hand and caught him. 'You of little faith,' he said, 'why did you doubt?'"*
>
> **Matthew 14:31 (NIV)**

Did you catch what Jesus said? Never did He say that Peter had no faith; He said that Peter had "little faith!" Friend, that's good news for you and me. Why? Because even with "little faith," Peter still did what no one else accomplished. He did the miraculous!

The point is clear: Never devalue your "little." In the pursuit of your dream, there will be times when you've emptied everything, leaving very little energy left in your tank. Don't underestimate what God can do with that small remnant of strength. You may have a little stature, be in a little building, starting a little business, live in a little town, and have little faith and little re- sources; but *thank God for what you have now*. When you do, God can turn your "little" into something great . . .

. . . For His glory and honor.

STAY EMPTY MY FRIENDS

For so long, I've thought the widow woman's miracle was in the filling of her empty jars, but that's only part of the story. The supernatural element of her miracle began when she obeyed the Word of the Lord and *emptied* out what she had.

... the Bible was never written to make sense; it was written to activate faith!

The catalyst for the supernatural is still the same today.

One of the key ways to experience the miraculous is by emptying yourself of anything and everything that stands in the way of God's power. Just think what could happen if you came to a place of total surrender and trust in your Savior? You don't have to know all of the answers and reasons why God has called you to certain places and to do certain things. All you need to know is that your Redeemer lives; and the more empty you are, the more He can bring His dream for your life alive.

There's no better place to be!

In the natural, the miracle of emptiness makes no sense whatsoever; but the Bible was never written to make sense; it was written to activate faith! Proverbs 3:5 says that we should trust in the Lord with all our heart and lean not on our own understanding. Since starting our church, we have emptied our bank account six times! That's right, six times. Every time, it was an act of faith. Most of the time, we were scared to death, but God honored our faith and our emptiness with supernatural abundance.

Your miracle hinges on first being empty. To see the supernatural power of God at work in your life, you must always make the first move. He's God, and He's been God longer than you've been you; so He calls the shots! But, He always has your best interest in mind. Would your Heavenly Father EVER lead you to a place of emptiness which He hasn't already provided a more than enough miracle? No way. That's not how your Abba Father operates. The Bible says that if we who are evil know how to give good gifts to our earthly children, how much more does our Heavenly Father give good things to us, His children — good measure, pressed down, and running over![4] That's just His nature.

When I finally came to the realization that God didn't need me and my great abilities (yeah, right) to make our church succeed, the pressure to perform was lifted. I came to this stark revelation: God can do whatever He wants with or without me! It's not my church, it's HIS church. In the same light, it's not your business, it's HIS business that you've been given the opportunity to oversee and steward. Just like John the Baptist described his relationship with Jesus, for Him to increase, you must decrease.[5]

Living a life of emptiness can be costly. When Jesus

was nearing the time of His death, a woman with an alabaster box full of priceless perfumes broke her jar and *emptied* what she had on Him.[6] Was that easy? No. It was a sacrifice. I can speak from experience, that when you empty yourself in a sacrificial way — a way that hurts and goes against everything you can rationalize in your mind — you are posturing yourself for a supernatural encounter with God. Pastor Mike Hayes once told me something that has rang in my spirit for years. He said:

"God always responds to sacrifice,
and He always pays back with interest."

God *always* responds to sacrifice. It's not about what you have; it's about what you don't have and what you're willing to give up. When God asks you (and He will . . . more than once), "What do you have in your hand?" it's a trick question! If your answer is anything except "Only you, Jesus," then it's time to examine yourself. The beauty of emptiness is this: realizing that nothing or nobody can provide for you like your Heavenly Father. No one can fill your life like He can. No one.

> The day you stop emptying yourself is the day the anointing will stop flowing in your life.

But, you must be empty.

As long as the widow and her sons had empty jars, the oil kept flowing. Oil in the Old Testament represents the Holy Spirit. Today, we are the jars. The day you stop emptying yourself is the day the anointing will stop flowing in your life. I can't think of a better reason to stay empty.

Emptiness is the womb for miracles. If God can get you to the place of emptiness, good things are on your horizon. Are you ready to empty yourself of your pride? Your ego? Your agenda? Your false sense of security? Your natural abilities and talents? Whatever God is asking you to empty yourself of, you can be sure that His provision is waiting in the wings. You're positioned for a miracle of epic proportion.

Welcome to the miracle of emptiness.

Chapter 5

STIRRING THE WATERS

You can't imagine how much I wanted to be a, "We started with nothing and within one year were busting at the seams," story; but we weren't. Actually, it was quite the opposite. One year after Leann and I had sold everything and headed to our "Promised Land," we were desperate. All of our efforts had produced very little fruit, both in the church and personally. We were in a financial and emotional mess with our backs literally against the wall. Something had to give. For us to continue this journey, a major change had to take place.

Never will I forget the moment—when counting our losses and closing the doors was making more sense every day—when the unexpected happened. God began to stir my heart. I couldn't put my finger on exactly what He was saying, so I began to pray, "God, what's this I feel? What are You doing in me?" After I prayed, I knew one place I could find my answer—in the Word.

The Lord led me to a passage, John 5:1-9, which I had read a hundred times; but this time, it made the most sense.

> "After this there was a feast of the Jews, and Jesus went up to Jerusalem. Now there is in Jerusalem by the Sheep Gate a pool, which is called in Hebrew, Bethesda, having five porches. In these lay a great multitude of sick people, blind, lame, paralyzed, waiting for the moving of the water. For an angel went down at a certain time into the pool and stirred up the water; then whoever stepped in first, after the stirring of the water, was made well of whatever disease he had. Now a certain man was there who had an infirmity thirty-eight years. When Jesus saw him lying there, and knew that he already had been in that condition a long time, He said to him, 'Do you want to be made well?'
>
> The sick man answered Him, 'Sir, I have no man to put me into the pool when the water is stirred up; but while I am coming, another steps down before me.'
>
> Jesus said to him, 'Rise, take up your bed and walk.' And immediately the man was made well, took up his bed, and walked."

When I read these scriptures, the irritation in me changed to a holy expectation. What I didn't know then, I know now. Just like this pool, the waters inside my heart were stirring! Something was moving. Something was shifting. Something was changing. God was preparing us to go to another level! But, for me to grasp what He was saying, I had to dig a bit deeper.

That's when it all started coming together.

ANGELS ON ASSIGNMENT

One of the first things that stands out in this passage is who actually came and stirred the waters — an angel. The original text actually says that as they came "to agitate" or "to disturb" the water, it was a sign to everyone around the pool that a miracle was on its way! Of course, this was biblical times, but what about today? Are angels still at work? Is there such a thing as angelic intervention in our lives? With everything that's in me, I resound a compelling, "Yes!" Angels are still at work today.

In the book of Revelation, John was in the spirit on the Lord's Day when Jesus gave him specific directions: "What you see, write in a book, and deliver it to the seven churches which are in Asia."[1] John obeyed the Lord's commands, but look to whom those letters were addressed: "To the angel at the church of . . . ."[2] This heavenly activity hasn't stopped. Just like in the book of Revelation, angels are still on assignment today. That's not spooky; it's a great thing! In the pursuit of your dream, you're never alone. There's an angel with specific functions from God assigned to you.

Friend, if you don't believe in the biblical activity of angels, I would suggest changing your theology very quickly. Hollywood has tried its best to lull us to sleep with television shows like *Touched by an Angel*, *Angels in the Outfield*, and *Charlie's Angels*! The city of Los Angeles is even called the "City of Angels." (That's a hard one to figure out!) Angels are real and are working right this very moment. Your angel could be stirring your waters right now.

You don't want to miss it!

THE BALANCING ACT

Wouldn't it be great if angels stirred the waters of miracles 24/7? We'd all love it! But, that's not how the Bible says they function. According to John 5:4, they only came at a "certain time." Other translations say a "certain season," not once a week, once a month, or on any certain time schedule; the angel only appeared during set seasons. Recognizing these seasons of divine intervention is so critical to the success of your dream.

Everything about life revolves around seasons. There are four seasons of the year, unless, of course, you live in Alaska or Florida! We have rainy seasons and dry seasons. People celebrate the Christmas season. Sports teams play a certain amount of games in a season. Life, in general, flows in seasons—some great, some not so great. In the pursuit of your dream, there will be times when the blessings of God seem to flow non-stop, while other periods are hard and dry. It's called "life!" After walking through some of these seasons myself and helping many others in their journey, one valuable lesson I've learned is this: Never be too excited about your good seasons, nor too discouraged in your bad seasons.

> Never be too excited about your good seasons, nor too discouraged in your bad seasons.

Like the ocean, life will always have ebbs and flows. When you experience a high season of life, don't become overly excited; that's a setup to be blindsided by your enemy. Even great of men of God in the Bible fell victim to this very trap. One, in particular, stands out—the Prophet Elijah.

In 1 Kings 18, Elijah was used mightily by God to defeat 450 prophets of Baal. Not only did Elijah experience a great victory, but God ended a severe drought over the land. Elijah was the hero of the day and God's man of faith and power . . . until the very next chapter.

Not everyone was happy about Elijah's great victory, including a woman named Jezebel. Her anger raged to the point where she issued a death sentence on Elijah's life. His reaction? God's man of "faith and power" took off running, hid under a tree, and begged God to kill him! This is the same man who had just killed 450 vicious warriors all by himself. It's true: Becoming too excited in a victory can be a set up for a setback.

Stay faithful and balanced in the season you're in. I've heard Pastor Mike Hayes say, "If the tires on your car aren't balanced, you're not going anywhere." What a true statement for tires and life. Balance is the key. Seasons will come and go. Things will change. People will fade in and out. Stay in the middle of the road. Your season will change. Be ready.

Your waters could be stirred at any moment!

TURNING THE TABLES

Being in youth ministry taught me the importance of strong relationships with the local school administration. I learned that if they liked me and felt as though we were all on the same team, they would give me the shirt off their back. Knowing the importance of these relationships, I quickly set an appointment to meet with one of the upper Forney school officials as soon as we arrived in town. Boy, was I ever in for a surprise.

I arrived a bit early and this man invited me into his office. The minute I walked in, he turned and closed the door behind us. (I knew that probably wasn't a good sign!) As I made my way over to sit in one of his office chairs, he barked, "I didn't say you could sit there, did I?" That was the highlight of our meeting! Before I could barely say, "Hello," and introduce myself, this man had started ripping me up one side and down the other. He bullied me our entire meeting! I never figured out why he was so mad at me. After all, we had only been in town for two weeks. Whatever the reason, he definitely let me know his opinions, which weren't pretty.

When this man finally finished verbally assaulting me, I gladly left his office. My emotions were so wrecked that I almost started to cry. I began to think *Man, I should've taken that old man down and given him what he deserved!* But, I knew that wouldn't be the right thing to do, especially since we were starting a church! I had to take his tongue lashing and move on; but it wasn't easy. Needless to say, our relationship with the Forney school administration didn't start out like I'd envisioned, but it was just a season . . . and seasons change.

A few years later, this same man was fired from his position due to his belligerence towards his staff. (Go figure!) After he was out of the picture, it wasn't long before the school principals, teachers, and administration welcomed us with open arms. Today, the school district treats Leann and I with the upmost respect; and we are working together to reach our community like never before. How did it change? At the right season, the angel came to stir the waters and God completely turned this situation around for our favor.

There have been so many times where God has turned the tables for our good. Another incident happened at my all-time favorite restaurant.

CHRISTMAS MIRACLE

It's no secret; I love Chic-fil-A®! You can imagine my excitement when I found one in our little town of Forney! (Actually, I think it was a confirmation from God that we had moved to the right place!) It didn't take long for the managers and employees to know me on a first name basis, since I visited that store practically every day for months. One day after finishing my meal, I handed someone in the restaurant an invitation to visit our new church. It wasn't a Gospel track; it was simply an invitation. The manager saw me and quickly asked that I not solicit the church in the restaurant. I was a bit taken back because, after all, Chic-fil-A® is a Christian company that's closed on Sundays! But, I honored his request and stopped. It was just a season.

Our time was coming.

Fast-forward three years. During the Christmas season, the same manager of that store called our office and asked if our music team could come on a Friday night and sing some Christmas songs . . . right in the middle of the store. That's right, the same place that had banned me from handing out invitations three years prior was now asking us to do Christmas songs on their busiest night of the week! We accepted their gracious invitation and the response was amazing. That night, we reached far more people than all of my efforts of handing out individual invitations combined. Everybody loved it. Even the manager commented on how glad he was we were there. I think I responded by ordering another chicken sandwich!

The point is this: Seasons change. At a certain season, an appointed time, God will send an angel to stir the waters of miracles. Get ready.

Good things will follow.

GETTING GOD'S ATTENTION

Recognizing the seasons of stirring is important, but it's only the first step. You must take corresponding action. The Bible says that when the angel stirred the water, not everyone responded. Even Jesus walked right through the very midst of the crowd, and they remained sick. All He had to do was speak the Word and every single one of them would've been healed, but He didn't. Why? Here lies another vital key for receiving your miracle in the season of stirring.

The Bible says that Jesus *saw* a *certain man*, lame for thirty-eight years, lying by the pool. Somehow, he knew this was his open window for a miracle, and he made the most of it. The results? He was completely healed. I believe this man taught a principle that's still true today: When your waters are stirring, you must recognize your opportunities.

In other words, you must get God's attention.

In Mark 5, there was a woman with a severe sickness who heard Jesus, the Healer, was coming to town. The crowds surrounded Jesus on every side that day, but she was not a normal bystander. This woman knew the waters were stirring, and she decided to get God's attention. Pressing through the crowd, she touched the bottom of Jesus' garment. Her results? She was completely healed. Her waters were stirring, and she took full advantage.

Mark 10, records a story of a blind beggar named Bartimaeus. As Jesus and the disciples came through the city, Bartimaeus, even though he was blind, knew his miracle was close. The waters were stirring. He began to yell, "Jesus, Son of David. Have mercy on me!"[3] Being an outcast of society, the crowd warned him to stay quiet and leave Jesus alone; but his desire to be healed outweighed their demands. He then yelled even louder, "Son of David, have mercy on me!"[4] Bartimaeus was determined to get Jesus' attention, no matter what it cost—and it worked. "Blind" Bartimaeus walked away as "healed" Bartimaeus.

The Bible doesn't say how the lame man by the pool caught Jesus' eye, but here's what we do know: He received what others didn't. No matter what everyone else did or didn't do, this man wasn't going to be denied. The same is true for you: Your future is not dependent upon those around you.

Your dream is not reliant upon other people's opinions.

Your dream is not reliant upon other people's opinions. When the waters are stirring, get God's attention—even while others sit around and miss out on their miracle. The question is simply this: What are you doing to get your Father's attention?

Your miracle depends on it.

EXCUSES OR ACTION

When the waters were stirred and this lame man did something for Jesus to take notice, he then hears Jesus ask a question that was music to his ears: "Do you want to be made well?" Isn't it interesting that Jesus gave him a choice? Now, the decision was up to him—excuses or action.

The very first thing out of this man's mouth was, "I don't have anyone to help me. I can't get into the pool by myself. Someone is always passing me by." Are you kidding me? A simple, "Yes!" would've done the trick! Of course, it's easy for you and me to play armchair quarterback and say, "Man, this is JESUS talking to you. Stop making excuses. Get up and get your miracle!" But, how many times have we been guilty of this exact, same thing? How many times has God asked us, "Do you want your miracle?" and we've responded with a laundry list of excuses? To add insult to injury, we have the Bible, full of God's promises and faithfulness; still, excuses seem to run rampant.

When you boil it all down, the lame man's excuse was one you still hear today: "Other people always pass me by." Man, oh man, have you ever felt that it was "your time," but someone else passed you by? Did someone else get a promotion while you stayed in your same position? Maybe you've been single for years, believing God to send the right mate, and your friend met and married their "dream" in a matter of months! Believe me, there's nothing quite as bad as feeling that God has passed you by. But, let me tell you; it's a trick of your enemy.

There have been times when I've looked at some pastors—a few who were barely potty-trained when I started in the ministry—and their churches are filled with thousands of people in just a few short years. In some ways, it seems that God has passed me by and someone else jumped in the waters before me. It's during these times that I usually start to reason (or rather, whine) with God about why I should be the one pastoring thousands. I'm quick to remind God how I've been faithful to serve Him in every way I know, how I've fasted and prayed, how I've committed my whole life to the ministry, blah, blah, blah. Really, there are two words that best describe my actions: pity party!

And, I'm the only one invited.

In the journey of your dream, playing the comparison game, even though it's human nature, is detrimental and often deadly. The truth is, some people will always seemingly pass you by, but how you celebrate other people's successes can determine how soon you will celebrate your own!

> . . . how you celebrate other people's successes can determine how soon you will celebrate your own!

Here's a thought. When you see someone accomplish their dream quicker or with more effectiveness than what you've experienced, why not use it as a motivation for your own personal growth? Change "God's forgotten about me" to "If God did it for them, I know He'll do it for me!" Try it. I can attest that this one simple shift in your thinking will accelerate you to your dream even quicker.

If you're a business owner who works tirelessly while others seem to play around all week, only work a few hours a day, and yet their businesses are growing by leaps and bounds, rejoice with their success. If you're a college student who studies all hours of the night to make B's and C's and your roommate hardly ever cracks open a book and has a 4.0 GPA, rejoice with their accomplishments. Maybe your goal is to be a stay-at-home mom and other women around you have been blessed with that opportunity while you're still having to go into work every day. Rejoice with them. If your family is struggling financially and others are being blessed, celebrate with them. The Bible says to rejoice with those who rejoice.[5] Why? Because it's true that what God's done for others, He will do for you.

No more excuses! It's time to act.

STIR IT UP!

When I say that after our first year our backs were against the wall, I am not kidding! It was one of the driest, most non-productive times of our ministry life. Everything seemed to be growing stale. We knew we had obeyed God, but things weren't clicking. Circumstances that would've normally been easy were now very difficult. Very solvable situations had escalated into major issues. It was during this time I felt God stirring the waters in my heart. I knew we couldn't stay in our current condition, so instead of making excuses, I acted.

One day, during this dry spell, I was spending time with the Lord in my personal sanctuary (a.k.a. my truck). I drove, prayed, worshiped, and most importantly, listened to what He had to say. Oh, there's one more thing I did that day. I asked God to show me houses that were for sale! This particular day, He did. The waters were stirring.

It was time to act.

While driving out in the country, I came upon a house for sale that also sat on some acreage. I went and asked the owner the sales price. He said $189,000 for the house and land. I quickly offered him $100,000! He looked at me and said, "Do you know what this house is worth? The lowest I can do is $150,000." So, I said, "Ok, how about $125,000?" The owner said "$135,000." I stayed quiet for a bit, and then he said, "Okay, $125,000 it is!" I was so excited; but my next order of business was to convince Leann and our daughters what a great deal we had made.

Again, I prayed!

We closed on the house and land a few weeks later and before the ink could dry on the contracts, I drove out to the property and put up a "For Sale" sign on the two acres adjacent to the house. The very next day, the lady who lived next door came and asked me, "What are you planning to do with this property?" I simply said, "I'm going to sell it." "How much?" she asked. "$50,000" I replied. Without much conservation, she bought the two acres that night! In just a little over twenty-four hours, we had already recouped forty percent of our investment. Action was paying off.

Leann and the girls aren't exactly what you'd call "country folk," so persuading them to move out to the country was a challenge. However, they finally agreed, and we moved—but the For Sale sign stayed in the yard from the moment we arrived! Five weeks after moving in, we left for our annual family vacation to Disney World in Florida. While on vacation, I received a call from a lady who was very interested in purchasing the house. We worked out a price over the phone and she bought it. A few weeks later (much to the joy of my wife and daughters), we closed on the house and within less than two months, we profited over $63,000 on our little house in the country investment.

Thank God we acted.

GET THEE BEHIND ME!

Another one of our "stirring of the waters" moments was not only an incredible stretch for us, but one of the most amazing miracles we've ever experienced.

During the church's first five years, we moved and changed locations so many times that we should've been called "Church on the Go!" We started in a small conference room, then moved to a school, then to another school, then to a movie theater, then back to another school, then into a rented building, and then into the facilities we currently occupy. The way we even landed in this building was a total God-deal but what happened before we even moved in was nothing short of miraculous.

Purchasing and remodeling our current building practically cost us everything. About two months before we moved in, our bank account was down to about $12,000. From this, we had to cover payroll for the week, pay the mortgage on the building, continue the remodeling, plus pay all of our other weekly expenses. We were at our financial limit. Just then, we were about to be stretched beyond our wildest imagination.

Right at this same time, I attended a pastor's conference in our area. During one of the sessions, the speaker stated that he was planting a church in another state. As soon as he finished the session, the leader of the conference then asked the attendees to sow financially into this new church launch. At first I thought *Oh, how nice! Why didn't anyone do that for us?* Then, the Lord began to speak to my heart. The waters were stirring.

Sitting in the auditorium, the Lord said, "Richie, I want you to give $10,000 toward this new church." What? Surely this must be the devil, since God knew we only had $12,000 to our name . . . with bills to pay! I wanted to say, "Get thee behind me, Satan," but I knew this was the leading of the Holy Spirit. Before jumping out into the deep, I called our CFO and said, "Man, you better be sitting down because you're either going to think I've lost my mind or you're going to go with me on this. I am about to give $10,000 out of our church account towards a new church plant."

Chirp. Chirp.

"Hello? Are you still there?"

The silence on the phone was deafening for a few seconds, then our CFO said, "Pastor, if that's what God's telling you to do, then go for it. He will provide."

The truth is, they really didn't need our offering almost $200,000 was raised in that one setting. Our giving wasn't going to make that much of a difference, but the waters were troubled, and we needed to get God's attention. When we did, the windows of Heaven opened!

Ten days after this event, a man I'd never seen before came to our church and gave an offering—a $100,000 offering! Not only that, over the next few weeks, he gave another $100,000. In all, this total stranger gave $200,000 to our church! Then, it broke loose. Two people gave $25,000 each; four gave $10,000 each; and several more gave $5,000 and $1,000 offerings. This was a financial harvest like we'd never experienced—ever! Up until this time, if someone would've given a $500 offering, I would've ran around the church and shouted at the top of my lungs! Now, just a few weeks after we gave

$10,000 towards the church plant, almost $500,000 was given to our church. It was insane!

The waters were stirred and we responded with action that grabbed God's attention; but the offering was only part of what God required. Looking back, it was probably the easiest part. A few days after we gave our offering, and before anyone had given a dime to us, God started dealing with me about another area, which I needed to respond for us to receive His outpouring. I firmly believe that taking this step, along with our offering, unlocked the heavens and allowed God to pour out a major blessing on us.

The Lord strongly laid on my heart to write a letter to a few families who had left our church. In this letter, I asked them to forgive me and/or the church for anything we had done to cause harm or offense. My motives were pure, as I wasn't attempting to win these people back; I was simply obeying God. Whether they received it in that fashion or not wasn't the issue; I did what God directed me to do, and it placed us in a position to receive an abundant blessing.

Once again, actions produced a harvest.

JUMP IN!

When the waters are stirred, jump in and ask God for the hard things. Believe for financial miracles, marriage restoration, and family members to be brought to Jesus.

Be quick to do whatever it takes to get God's attention. God might have you do something that seems crazy or is very difficult. Whatever the case may be, don't make excuses. Act on it, and then get ready for Him to open the windows of Heaven.

Above all, keep your confession right. I truly believe that positive confessions activate angelic action in your life, while negative confessions release demonic activity, bringing confusion and disarray.

There was a particular time I found this to be true.

As we were preparing to remodel our new building, I was jogging one day and saw what looked like a hand hanging over our congregation. It was releasing things in the spirit to our church. At the risk of sounding like a nutcase, I nervously began speaking what I saw—while jogging! I said out loud, "I see a supernatural release coming to this church." "Release," seemed crazy at the time, but I kept declaring it; and in only two weeks, we received all of the resources needed to cover the remodel of our building—every single dime. With these gifts, we were able to occupy the building and open as scheduled. It's true that if you say what you hear, you will see what you said.

> . . . if you say
> what you
> hear, you will
> see what you
> said.

Don't be afraid to jump into the waters and boldly confess what you're believing God to do. Jeremiah 33:3 says to ask God, and He will show you great and mighty things that you don't even know currently exist. That's how much God loves you and is committed to make sure your dream—His dream for you—comes to pass. The waters are stirring! You better get ready, because when they stir, it means one thing . . .

. . . A supernatural outpouring is on the way!

Chapter 6

DIVINE COUNTERBALANCE

While sitting in the parking lot of our local Star-bucks®, waiting on a couple with whom I was doing pre-marital counseling, I called my mom just to check on her. When she answered the phone, she was crying. I could tell something was desperately wrong. At first, I thought her mother, my grandmother, who had been very ill of late, had gone to be with Jesus. A part of that assumption was true. In fact, someone had gone to Heaven that day; but it wasn't my grandmother.

My mom frantically said, "Richie, has anyone called you today?" I said, "No, Mom. What's up?" Then, she uttered the words that completely blindsided me. "Richie, your daddy's been killed in a car wreck." At that very moment, my mind began to process the horri-fying news that was just delivered to me. Instantly, all the air seemed to be sucked out of my body. It felt as though my life had hit the pause button. Life as I knew it would be altered forever.

Leann, our girls, and I left Texas as quickly as we could and headed to Georgia to be with my mom and our family. When the news started to spread, the outpouring of love and support through phone calls, text messages, and practically every source of social media was overwhelming. Our hearts were so touched and comforted in our time of grief. I really don't know how we would've made it without the love shown from God's people.

While every card, call, text, and post meant so much to us, one message stood out to me. It wasn't just a note of condolence, but was also a prophetic word of direction, encouragement, and instruction. The morning of my father's funeral, which was also my and Leann's sixteenth wedding anniversary, I was awakened by a text message from a friend of mine in South Texas. It read:

> *"Good morning, Richie. My heart hurts for you and your family. I'm reminded of what I felt when my father unexpectantly went home to be Jesus. I was shocked and in disbelief and had an overwhelming need to talk to him, knowing I had been promoted to a new rank, personally. I'm praying for you and want you to know that God will help you and your family through this. Everything will be okay, Richie. God will bring all the pieces together. For He is*

*the God of **divine counterbalance**. When we
lose on one hand, He will do something wonderful on the other hand to compensate for your
loss. Expect really good things to happen. Know
that I love you, Richie, and admire your ministry."*

As I was reading this message, one phrase really
stood out to me that I had never heard before: "divine
counterbalance." Something about those two words spoke
to my heart, and I knew they were more than just a cute,
Christian cliché. They had a deep spiritual meaning, and
I knew I must search them out further.

IN A NEW LIGHT

Webster's Collegiate Dictionary defines the word "counterbalance" as: *"A weight that balances another; a force or influence that offsets or checks an opposing force."* Reading this
excited my heart, as I knew God was about to offset my
loss with something amazing! He was sending a balance
to weigh against our tragedy, and it was going to be
good — really good.

Now I needed to know what this entire phrase,
"divine counterbalance," meant, spiritually — and what
better place to research something "divine" than the
Bible, right? That's exactly where I looked.

In all my years of being in church and the ministry,

I'd never seen nor heard of anything like this phrase in the Bible. Quite honestly, I wondered if there even was such a thing in the Scriptures. Thank God I looked! It didn't take long to find a very familiar passage which ended my search:

> *"Come to Me, all you who labor and are heavy laden, and I will give you rest. Take My yoke upon you and learn from Me, for I am gentle and lowly in heart, and you will find rest for your souls. For My yoke is easy and My burden is light."*

> **Matthew 11:28-30**

If you're like me, you've probably heard these words of Jesus many times. But, I want to bring your attention to one word that, when you understand its original meaning, will cause you to see these scriptures in a totally different light. It's the word: "yoke."

The word, "yoke," as found here in verse twenty-nine, is translated from the Greek word *zygos*, which literally means "a balance, a pair of scales."[1] Knowing this meaning, can you see what Jesus was saying concerning our struggles and battles in life? In our modern-day vernacular, His message would sound something like this:

*"When you're burdened down by life, take My yoke on
you. Why? Because your enemy has not had the last
word in your life! It's not over until I say it's over!
There's something working in your favor to balance
out what has been taken and stolen from you!"*

Here's good news. Whatever has you burdened: dif-
ficulty in a marriage, a struggle with a teenager; loss of
a job; or maybe, like me, you've lost a loved one in an
untimely death — God, the Great Equalizer, is at work
weighing out the balance for your favor! Maybe your
life-dream seems to be over. If so, let me tell you something that you should never forget: No matter what it
looks like, with God, it's never over until He says it's
over!

His divine counterbalance is at work.

THE LAST WORD

One of the most powerful counterbalances God uses is
His grace. Look how *The Message* Bible translates this same
passage in Matthew 11:

> *"Are you tired? Worn out? Burned out on
> religion? Come to me. Get away with me,
> and you'll recover your life. I'll show you
> how to take a real rest. Walk with me and
> work with me — watch how I do it. Learn
> the unforced rhythms of grace . . . "*

Look at the last phrase: ". . . *the unforced rhythms of grace!*" I don't know about you, but I've been a recipient of God's unforced rhythms of grace many, many times in my life, especially during seasons when I was carrying heavy burdens and weights. It was in those times that the grace of God picked me up and carried me through to better days. It's nothing new; God's grace has been balancing the scales from Bible days.

Joseph, the "dreamer," was threatened to be killed and eventually sold into slavery by his own brothers. Surely, he must have questioned God in all of the unjust actions dealt towards him. But, it didn't matter if Joseph was in the bottom of a well, in a pit, in prison, or if he was being falsely accused by his boss' wife; God's grace was balancing the scales in his favor. In the end, Joseph was promoted to serve as the vice-president of the country, and his testimony was, *"What my enemy meant for destruction, God, by His amazing grace, turned it for my good."*[2] God's grace had the last word.

Job was a man of great fortune, only to lose everything within a short amount of time. His life turned so dark that his wife, who blamed God for all his misfortune, begged Job to curse God and die.[3] But, Job believed differently. Instead of acting on his wife's ill-advised suggestion, Job looked to God as His deliverer. A divine counterbalance was working in Job's favor, and he was restored with a double portion of everything he had lost.

One of the greatest examples of God's grace, working to balance the scales, was in the death and resurrection of Jesus. Here was a man who never sinned, yet He was abused, betrayed, falsely accused, beaten, condemned, and unjustly murdered. I've often wondered what took place in hell the day Jesus was crucified. I'm sure the devil himself and all of his demon cohorts were ecstatic, knowing that their arch enemy, Jesus, was out of the way — dead, buried, and gone forever . . . or, so they thought.

The story wasn't over.

Even though Friday (the day Jesus was crucified) looked dim, Sunday was on the way! God's amazing grace stepped in and said, "It's not over." After three days in the grave, Jesus rose from the dead; taking with Him the keys of death, hell, and the grave.[4] Now, due to that divine counterbalance; today, we say as the Apostle Paul did, "Death, where is your sting? Hell, where is your victory?"[5]

Grace had the final word.

God's grace hasn't changed. It's still available for you today. For example:

- Weeping may last for a night, but joy — **grace** — comes in the morning.[6]

- The afflictions of the righteous are many, but God's **grace** delivers them from them all.[7]

- A righteous man falls seven times in a day, but the **grace** of God will pick him up every time.[8]

No matter what you're going through, now or in the future, one thing is for certain: Grace always has the last word, even if you don't feel like you deserve it!

ONE FOR THE AGES

If you know anything about the nature of God, it's fairly easy to comprehend His grace covering you for mistakes you've unknowingly made. But, what about the hardships you've endured as result of *your* actions? Believe me, we've all made decisions which have produced costly mistakes. But in the end, God's grace—not your mistakes in life—is what defines you. It's not over until God says it's over.

> . . . in the end, God's grace—not your mistakes in life—is what defines you.

The life of Peter, one of Jesus' disciples, is a great example.

While Peter was passionate for the Lord, he also had a life full of faults and failures. The night Jesus was arrested by the Roman soldiers in the Garden of Gethsemane, Peter let his anger get the best of him; and he chopped off a soldier's ear.[9] Then, he succumbed to the pressure of even knowing Jesus and openly denied Him three times.[10] On one occasion, when Peter suggested that Jesus not go to the cross, Jesus rebuked him by saying, "Get behind me, Satan."[11] Being called "Satan" by Jesus probably wasn't the highlight of Peter's ministry resume; but even so, his life wasn't over. Grace was at work.

After Jesus arose from the dead, He showed Himself to His disciples on numerous occasions. They were all ecstatic to see their Master alive . . . all except one: Peter. Maybe he, much like many others today, was convinced he'd done too much wrong to be associated with the Master. Surely, he felt disqualified through his actions to be in Jesus' presence. Whatever the case, Peter was about to experience one of the greatest divine counterbalances ever recorded in the Bible.

Not long after Jesus' resurrection, He had an encounter with Peter, in which Jesus asked him the same question three times: "Peter, do you love Me?" Peter's answer to all three questions, "Yes."[12] A few days after this encounter, 120 Believers were gathered in an Upper Room on the Day of Pentecost, awaiting the outpouring of the Holy Spirit, just as Jesus had promised. After they were all baptized in the Holy Spirit, guess who led the charge to spread the news? Peter. History records that Peter was the first person in the Church to ever preach a sermon—and the results were amazing! The Bible says that when he finished, 3,000 people were saved![13] Not only was this event the supernatural start of the Church, but it was also God's counterbalance at work. Here's how:

Action:
Peter denies Jesus three times.

Counterbalance #1:
Jesus gave him three opportunities to voice his love for Him.

Counterbalance #2:
God gave him 3,000 souls in return!

For every time Peter denied the Lord, God gave him a thousand souls! Now, THAT'S what you call divine. But, that's not all. Remember how Peter cut off the soldier's ear? God's counterbalance was anointing Peter with so much power that even when his shadow fell on people, they were healed.[14]

These same unforced rhythms of grace are weighing out the balance in your life, even though, at times, it may not seem so. You walk by faith, not by what you see.[15] No matter what you face or how much you feel you have failed God, never lose focus on this one fact: Grace always has the last say.

"YOU NEED US!"

In one of the churches where Leann and I were youth pastors, we had a married couple who not only served as key youth leaders, but were also substantial givers. In the beginning, it was a blessing to have them on our team, as oftentimes I needed approval for something and this man (who also served on the church's finance committee) would go to bat for us. During that time, we were approved for pretty much anything we needed. Things started out well, but unfortunately the relationship took a turn for the worse.

Once while on a youth trip, this man's wife became very offended at something and began to stir up all kinds of strife with other adult leaders. Knowing that it's always best to address situations like this early, I tried to pull her aside and talk out her issues; but she refused. Even after the trip was over, she continued to spew her poison on our leadership team, and it was getting ugly — really ugly. Something had to be done.

Our senior pastor heard of the conflict and requested a meeting with me and the couple. His motive was to hear what happened and come to a peaceful agreement, so we could all move forward. However, that's not quite how it ended.

During our meeting, things got heated — really heated. Every solution or resolution our pastor offered, they rejected. It came to the point that this couple was so offended, the only thing that would satisfy them was my resignation. (Really, she was offended, and her husband just borrowed her offense.) Knowing their position and financial contributions to the church, I wanted to make this whole ordeal as easy as possible for our pastor. So, right on the spot, in the middle of this discussion, I resigned and stood up to walk out the door. What happed next took me by surprise.

Before I reached the door, our pastor stood up and blocked the doorway and wouldn't let me leave! I asked, "Pastor, what are you doing? The best solution is for me to resign, and I need to leave now." He responded, "Richie, if you leave, you're going to have to go through me!" Needless to say, the meeting turned *very* interesting in a hurry. When this couple saw our pastor's commitment to me, they gathered their things and walked out in a huff. As they were leaving, the lady turned around and with a snarky tone said, "Well, I guess you'll see how much you need us!" This really didn't surprise me. For years, this woman's husband constantly reminded me of his prominent position in the church. He'd say things like, "Remember, I sign your checks!" Now, the impact of them actually leaving weighed heavily on my mind.

A few days later, the inevitable happened. The couple—and their financial support—left the church. Much to my surprise, our pastor didn't even try to stop them. Everyone knew the significance of their leaving, and we needed God to show up in a big way. We needed a divine counterbalance, and God sent one.

Up until this time, we had worked and worked with our teens and leaders to break the 150 attendance mark in our youth service, but it never happened . . . that is, until the next service following this couple's departure. That night, we set an attendance record! Two hundred and eighty-eight students attended our youth service that night. That might not seem like a very big deal to most; but for me, it was God's divine counterbalance at work!

From that time on, our youth ministry flourished and grew like we'd never seen. Our church as a whole grew. The finances grew. It was nothing short of a divine intervention from God. While I was so honored that our pastor stood up for me like he did, the most valuable lesson I learned through this was even more powerful:

Anyone can walk out, but as long as you still have God, He's all you need!

Grace always has the last word.

THE KEY WORD

Maybe you've been believing God for a divine turnaround for years, and it hasn't happened quite *yet*. Well, the most important word to that statement is the very last one: "YET!" That word makes every demon in hell tremble. Why? Because it's a recognition that you're waiting for your promise to be fulfilled at any moment. Your "yet" means that you're still believing, you're still trusting, you're still moving forward, and still walking in faith. You might not have your answer right now, but never let go of your "yet!"

Our church has grown supernaturally by the grace of God, for which I'm so thankful. However, I know we haven't even scratched the surface of what God has in store for us. We're still living in our "yet" and will be until Jesus comes. God has shown His hand at work so many times that giving up now would be completely foolish, because we haven't seen anything — yet!

Refuse to let your pain win. Instead, use your pain to plow the ground for your purpose.

Trials come and go, but the Word of God lives forever. You can never exalt your experiences or what you're going through over the Word of God. Why? Because what you are experiencing — good or bad — will pass. Refuse to let your pain win. Instead, use your pain to plow the ground for your purpose. You may have lost a little bit, but know that on the other side of the scales, God is weighing out everything for your victory. World renowned author and poet, Maya

Angelou, said it best:

> "We may encounter many defeats,
> but we must never ever be defeated."

God's going to settle the score. You could be in a life-defining moment right now. The passing of my father was one of those moments for me. During that time, I made a decision that instead of being buried in grief and sorrow and weighed down with care and worry, I was going to rely on God's divine counterbalance which was working on the other side of the scale. I made up my mind that, by the grace of God, I wasn't going to be the same person, the same husband, the same father, the same pastor or preacher that I had been up to that point. The enemy tried to take me out emotionally, spiritually, and physically, but that didn't happen. My pain became the breeding ground to my purpose.

You can't run so far away that the blood of Jesus can't rescue you or God's counter-balance can't find you.

God was loading the other side of the scales!

Don't stop praying. Don't stop believing in your dream. Keep your eyes on Jesus who is working on your behalf. He's sees your tears. He hears your prayers. He knows your heart. He authored your dream, and He will balance out the equation. You can't run so far away that the blood of Jesus can't rescue you or God's counterbalance can't find you. Your "yet" is coming. God is turning the tables. No matter what you go through, always remember God is the Great Equalizer, . . . and He's balancing the scales in your favor!

Chapter 7

PASSING THE TEST

Very rarely have I ever met anyone who isn't contending for the absolute best in their life. It's even more seldom that I meet a Christian who doesn't desire all that God has for them. I'm convinced that deep-rooted on the inside of every person is the God-given desire to do more, be more, and have more. Everyone desires to be blessed, favored, and promoted—and they should. God loves to bless His children.

One of the most quoted passages of scripture concerning blessings is Deuteronomy 28:3-13. People are quick to quote these verses over themselves and say, "I'm blessed in the city and in the country. I'm blessed going in and coming out. Everything I put my hands to is blessed," . . . and so on. Now, there's nothing wrong with confessing these things over your life. In fact, I would encourage you to do it daily, even multiple times a day. But, as you're confessing the blessings;

don't forget to back up to the *beginning* of the chapter. There, you'll find the key to this entire passage.

> *"If you fully obey the* LORD *your God and carefully follow all his commands . . . All these blessings will come on you and accompany you if you obey the* LORD *your God:"*

Deuteronomy 28:1-2 (NIV)

God has promised to bless His children; it's part of the everlasting covenant He originally made with Abraham. But, these blessings don't just come because you're a Christian. They are conditional. Before you can partake in the *rewards* laid out in verses three through thirteen, you first must meet the *requirements* established in verses one and two.

This isn't the only passage of Scripture where you see this principle. The Bible is full of conditional promises.

For example, God promises that He would supernaturally heal our land; but there are a few conditions to be met: (1.) We must be called by His name; (2.) we must humble ourselves; (3.) we must pray and seek His face; and (4.) we must turn from wickedness.

When we do these things, THEN God is bound by His Word to perform the promise—to hear from heaven, forgive our sin, and heal our land.[1] What an awesome promise from the Lord!

But, it's conditional.

In the same way, many Christians are believing God to bless them financially, "good measure, pressed down, shaken together, and running over."[2] This is a great promise, but it's conditional. The Bible says to receive this promise you must first, "Give and it shall be given to you . . ."[3] There's no "good measure, pressed down, shaken together, and running over" blessing headed your way, until you first meet the prerequisite.

Thank God that Jesus purchased and met all of the requirements for our salvation when He died on the cross and rose from the grave. Since the price for redemption is now paid in full, then why isn't everyone saved? The last part of John 3:16 gives the answer: the free gift of eternal life only comes to those who *believe*.

There are many other examples throughout the Bible. "*Ask* and you shall receive. *Seek* and you will find. *Knock* and the door will be opened."[4] "*If we confess* our sin, He is faithful to forgive us and cleanse us from all unrighteousness,"[5] . . . and so on.

Every promise from the Lord has a condition. Very rarely will God just "show up" and bless you. When you study the conditions for blessings, they all revolve around one word. It's the key that can launch you into a great promotion and success.

That one word is obedience.

PAVING THE WAY

Have you ever noticed how kids never have to be taught to disobey? Disobedience—from touching a hot stove, not doing homework, not taking a bath, and coming home after curfew—is inherently rooted in our nature. Hopefully, you were trained to obey your parents, your teachers, your elders, and the law (and have trained your own kids, if you have them);

Obedience paves the way for increase.

but there's something else of the upmost importance you must learn to obey, as well: God's Word. Is it easy? No, obedience—no matter to whom or what—is never easy; however, it paves the way for increase.

It's called "the obedience test."

There are many people in the Bible who had to pass the test of obedience, but when they did, God did something earth-shaking.

Noah—blind obedience. Blind obedience is obeying God when there's no logical reason to do so. Noah's responsibility wasn't to please his family or answer his critics; he only had to obey God. In the end, the whole earth was destroyed, but Noah and his family were saved. Sometimes, your obedience will not make any sense to those around you, especially those closest to you! But, no matter the opinions of others, you must pass the obedience test.

Abraham—full obedience. Genesis 22 recounts how the "Father of Faith" fully obeyed the Lord in taking his son, Isaac, to be sacrificed. Abraham didn't cut any corners in doing what God had asked him to do, as he took Isaac, a rope to tie him up with, a knife to kill him with, and enough wood to offer him as a burnt offering to the top of the mountain. When they reached their destination, Abraham never wavered. He built an altar, tied up his son, and laid him on the wood. (I wonder what was going through Isaac's mind at that moment!) Just as Abraham raised his knife to slay his son, God spoke, "Do not lay a hand on the boy."[6] I'm sure Isaac lifted up a massive shout of praise at that moment!

After Abraham had fully obeyed, God provided a miracle of provision. It's true, partial obedience is disobedience.

Jesus—complete obedience. Our Savior was the highest example of obedience, even as He was obedient to His own death on the cross.[7] Never was this so evident as His prayer in the Garden of Gethsemane just a few days before His brutal death. Facing the torture and anguish of crucifixion, Jesus, sweating drops of blood, asked the Father if there was another way to purchase mankind's salvation.[8] Jesus didn't stop there. He ended His prayer by saying:

". . . yet not my will, but yours be done."

Luke 22:42 (NIV)

Jesus passed the obedience test, and today we have direct access to the Father. The Bible also says that because of His obedience to the cross, God exalted Jesus to the highest place and gave Him a name that is above every name![9]

Obedience paves the way to blessing and promotion.

START SMALL

Now, before you start thinking, *"Hey, I'm not Noah, I don't have the faith of Abraham, and I'm surely not Jesus,"* let me put your mind at ease by saying God's probably not going to ask you to build an ark, sacrifice your first-born, or pay for the sins of the world! He will, however, test your obedience even in the small things. The obedience test almost always begins with simple issues. They might seem simple, but they're most certainly not insignificant. How you handle the simple tests of obedience will position you for greater miracles and greater blessings down the road.

What exactly do small tests of obedience look like? Maybe God has asked you to share the Gospel with a specific co-worker, to bless a neighbor who you really don't like, to lay down a pesky habit, or to read your Bible and pray every day. These are far from building an ark or sacrificing your son! Think about it, though. How can you expect God's supernatural blessings to overtake you when you can't pass the simple tests? Notice, I said, "Simple," not "Easy!" Sometimes the smallest acts of obedience require great faith and humility.

I've experienced many of these types of tests.

POOLSIDE DRAMA

A few summers ago, Leann and I took our girls down to our neighborhood pool for a swim. As soon as we settled in, a lady came over from out of the blue and started chewing me out! To this day, I'm not quite sure what her problem was with me, but she definitely had an issue . . . and she wasn't very nice.

The next day, Leann was out and about, so I took the girls back to the pool. As soon as the girls jumped in, I sat down and this time the lady's husband came over and confronted me! He proceeded to tell me how rude and disrespectful I was to his wife the day before. Now, Leann is usually the first one to tell me if I was rude to someone, but on this occasion, even she was quick to comment how rude this lady was to me. Immediately, I knew this guy was way off in his judgment, but I listened to his rant. To make things worse, all of his buddies were sitting across the pool watching the entire scene. Believe me, my male pride was running on high octane; and I *really* wanted to put this guy in his rightful place—and I had every right to do it, too . . . but something else rose up inside of me.

Instead of doing what I really felt like, I remained in my seat; and when he had finished, I said, "Sir, I'm so sorry." For a number of minutes, I apologized to this man, even asking him to bring his wife over, so I could sincerely apologize to her, as well. She came over and I asked for her forgiveness—all the time still wondering what in the world I did or said that so disrespected her. At that point, it didn't matter.

I was being tested.

The next day, Sunday, was July the Fourth. In Texas, many people take advantage of this holiday weekend by heading out to one of our many lakes to enjoy their family time together. As a young pastor, I was nervous about who would even show up on that Sunday. Much to my surprise, 566 people were in church that day. At that time, it was an all-time attendance record.

Now, you might think the timing of this break-through was purely circumstantial, but I know beyond a shadow of a doubt that what happened that Sunday was in direct response to my simple test of obedience at the pool the day before. Thank God I didn't respond the way I wanted to, but took the high road and displayed a Christ-like attitude. It was nothing more than a test.

Thank God I passed.

"WILL YOU DO IT"

A few years after our church was up and running, we started to outgrow our facility. Something had to change, so we sought out different ways to accommodate more growth. After much prayer, I felt led to look for another facility in a town about twenty-five minutes away to open a second campus. I put action to what God was saying and within a few weeks, we found a building.

Our Sunday services were already maxing out our volunteer staff, so, I decided to hold our second campus' service on Saturday nights. Quite honestly, the thought of doing another service, on another night of the week, was never really accepted by our leadership team; but I knew the Lord was leading us that direction. We launched our first Saturday night service at our second location, and it was well attended. This seemed like a great answer to our dilemma, but God had another plan.

It hinged on our obedience.

The Monday following our very first Saturday night service, a very wealthy man in our town whom I had known for a few years called me and said, "Richie, there's a furniture store in town that's going out of business and their building's going to be empty soon." I said, "Sir, thank you so much for thinking about us, but we aren't in a financial position to take over that building, plus the bank won't loan a new church that much operating capital." Without hesitation, this man said the words I will never forget, "Son, I AM THE BANK!"

What I didn't know is that this man *owned* that building and was willing to help us make the transition with very little money out of our pocket. If that wasn't amazing enough, he also loaned us $400,000 to complete all the building renovations! Within a few months, we shut down the Saturday night service and moved to our beautiful new facility, which we occupy to this day.

Looking back, I can see where the Lord never intended us to start a second location at that time; it was just an obedience test. In some ways, this scenario felt much like Abraham and Isaac; in that after we fully obeyed, the provision of the facilities we needed literally fell into our lap. God was simply asking, "Will you be willing to do it?" Our actions answered, "Yes," which positioned us to have more than we could've ever dreamed at the time. Like Abraham, we fully obeyed . . .

. . . And God honored it.

TWO MORE WAYS

Obedience comes from different ways and has many faces. Two of the most common ways that test our obedience are through faithfulness and trials. Let's take a look at each one.

Faithfulness. Faithfulness is what I call Obedience 101. It's the baby steps of following God. It never ceases to amaze me how many people say that they are *full of faith*, but they have no *faithfulness* in their lives! The bottom line on this issue is simple: You must be faithful to be full of faith.

Matthew 25 records a story told by Jesus of three servants who were each given a specific amount of money from their master. While their master went on a journey, two of the men were faithful to not only keep what they had been given, but they also doubled their money. Upon returning, the master was pleased with their diligence, and he said, "Well done, good and faithful servant; you were faithful over a few things, I will make you ruler over many things."[10]

Notice, he called them *faithful* servants. He never said, "Good and *successful* servants." Neither did he say, "Good and *prosperous* servants." No, these men were faithful with the little they were given; and because they exhibited Obedience 101, they were put in charge of many things! Promotion comes from obedience through faithfulness.

Trials. As much as you probably don't want to hear it, another way obedience comes is through the tests and trials of life. Every year, students in Texas take an end-of-the-year assessment test called the STAAR test. Before a child can be promoted into the next grade, they must pass this test. This is true in life, as well. You will be encountering storms and trials for as long as you live. It's part of life. However, how you choose to view these tests is up to you. You can see the storms of life as something that will *destroy* you or *promote* you. Either can be true; the choice is yours.

The next time you face a storm or trial, don't think that you're going under. Instead, know that your Father God knew it was coming, and He's qualifying you for promotion. Think of it this way. What kind of teacher gives their students a test, hoping they will fail? Not a very good one, that's for sure! It's the same way with God. Why would a loving, Heavenly Father, who willingly gave up His only Son to die for your sins, allow you to take a test, that He knew you would fail? He wouldn't.

Trials bring promotion.

It might seem like all hell is breaking loose at times, but at the end of every season of life, there's a test to see what you've learned during that season. If you pass the test, guess what awaits you on the other side? Promotion and blessing! Just hang on. You will pass the test.

Leann and I are living examples of how faithfulness and trials can move you into a place of blessing and promotion. Every time God has called us to something greater in life, He first gave us a test of obedience. And, just like you, in order for God to release us into our dream, we had to pass the test . . . every single time.

GOTTA SELL IT

When God spoke to us about starting our church, it was the biggest test of obedience we had ever encountered to that point. Everything was good where we were. In the natural, to load up the truck and head to Forney, Texas seemed ridiculous; but we knew God had spoken and our dream awaited our obedience.

One of the first tests we faced was the sale of my Hummer. (Talk about the ultimate test of faithful obedience!) Everyone knew I loved my Hummer; but with our relocation, a $638 per month car payment wasn't being a good steward of our limited resources. So, it had to go.

Since we lived in a smaller town and there weren't many Hummers on the market, I thought it would be a pretty easy sale. Wrong! Every avenue I tried produced no results. Finally, I went and asked a friend, who owned a car lot on the highway, if I could park it out front. He was gracious and allowed me to do so. After a few days on the lot, we still had no bites. I was beginning to get worried when the Lord gave me very specific instructions. He said, "Go lay your hands on your truck and pray in a buyer!" I immediately thought, *"How ridiculous can this be?"* It was a test of my obedience. That same night, I did exactly what God instructed me to do.

There I was, right on the highway with people passing by looking at me like I had lost my mind, laying my hands on my Hummer and praying OUT LOUD for a buyer! It was all I knew to do. The following day, I called the car lot and asked if anyone had stopped by to see it. Much to my surprise, the secretary said, "Yes, as a matter of fact someone is in here buying it *right now,* and they're paying *full price!"*

After it sold, my car lot friend told me, "Richie, you ought to be ashamed of yourself. Nobody pays that much for a Hummer these days!" What he failed to realize was that this Hummer was a very specific color which was almost impossible to find. Not only that, but it was the exact color the buyer was looking for! Thus, he paid top dollar for it.

We had passed the first test.

Now that my Hummer—and the $638 monthly payment—were gone, the next hurdle was selling our brand new custom-built home. This was more than just a house; it was a home Leann and I had designed for our family. We were so looking forward to celebrating our first Christmas in it, so to sell it was another huge test.

We put the "For Sale" sign in the yard and were expecting calls from potential buyers quickly. Wrong again! There was no activity for three full weeks, barely a phone call. We knew that selling our house was one of the major steps to us moving, so something had to give. We were running out of time. Once again, our obedience was being tested.

One day, I gathered Leann and the girls together and said, "Girls, this house has to sell, so we can move. We need to pray for the right buyer to come quickly." Right then, we came into agreement, as a family, for God to send the right buyer—but that wasn't all. I knew what happened after I laid my hands on my Hummer, so I suggested that our family go outside and do the same thing to our house. Leann immediately spoke up and said, "Richie, are you crazy?!" Okay, so that wasn't quite the response I was looking for, but our oldest daughter, Sydni, agreed to come out with me. (She probably felt sorry for me!) Just like the Hummer, we walked around the house, laid hands on it in broad daylight, and believed God to work a miracle—and He did.

Within an hour after we prayed, we were all eating at Chic-Fil-A® and a man called me to view the house. Two weeks later, they bought it for $8,000 more than its appraised value! The money we profited from the sale helped us to move and start the church.

Without a doubt, I loved my Hummer; and we loved our house, but God's bigger plan and dream for our lives was calling us to a deeper level of obedience. From the very beginning of this journey, God was testing us to see if we would respond in obedience. I firmly believe that our willingness to obey opened the door for our dream—and we've never looked back.

GIVE IT AWAY

I wish I could say that the obedience tests stopped after we moved into our God-given dream. Actually, it was quite the opposite! Over the years, God has required much more sacrifice from us in many different areas; but in the end, it always paid incredible dividends.

Two years after we started the church, our finances were so tight that I had to do something to earn extra money. Since high school, I'd always been in and around health clubs and was very familiar with that business. I started working at a gym in the tenth grade by "cleaning the chrome," which is basically a fancy phrase for wiping down the weights and bars! By the time I graduated high school, I was one of the top salespeople for new memberships. I've always loved that industry, so I did some research and found a small town about twenty minutes away that was a prime location for a health club. I put my plan together, gathered some investors, and we were on our way.

You must be faithful to be full of faith.

In January 2007, Reality Fitness opened the doors to an overwhelming response. Literally, before we could even blink, we had over 500 members! God truly blessed our efforts. Everyone was ecstatic (especially our investors), but I could quickly see how the business was a distraction to my dream. That left me with only one real solution: I had to sell the business. Some people thought I was crazy because of the income it was already generating, but I knew it had to be done. Within 120 days of opening, the health club sold; and after we paid our investors and accounted for all of the remodeling, we walked away with $90,000 profit!

Now the real test came.

God told us to give a significant amount of it back into the Kingdom!

By this time, we had already been through many tests of obedience, so we knew something great was waiting on the other side of our giving — but even then, it was hard to turn loose of that much money! Some people thought we were crazy. Their advice was, "Richie, you're young. Take that money, invest it, and let it grow to be your retirement one day." Now, having a retirement plan is good; but there's something even better — *obeying the voice of God.*

We did exactly what God said and gave a substantial amount back into the Kingdom. People shook their heads, as they couldn't understand our reasoning.

That wasn't the end of the story.

Fast forward one year, to 2008. That year, the U.S. economy crashed harder than it had since the Great Depression of the 1920's. In fact, I knew a person who, in one day, lost over a million dollars . . . in the very stock which we were advised to invest! Once again, obedience paid off and kept us from losing everything we had profited. The lesson we learned that day has stuck with us ever since: You never give to get; you give out of obedience.

Over and over again, it's so easy to see the hand of God in every step He has required of us. Many times, it seemed as though we had lost our minds and were following some crazy idea in our heads. It was in some of those moments that we were tempted to ignore the voice of God, but we didn't. Thank God, He's always been faithful to perform His Word and reward our obedience.

THREE REASONS

The benefits of passing the obedience test are numerous, but I believe three stand out.

> **Obedience proves faith**. There's an old adage that says, "Put your money where your mouth is." That simply means your beliefs need to be backed up by your actions. That's exactly what obedience allows you to do—to walk out the faith in which

you believe. Either you have faith, or you don't. Obedience will tell the tale.

Nineteenth century French tightrope artist, Charles Blondin, was a man who lived life on a wire. To this day, he still holds the world record for the number of times he walked a tightrope across Niagara Falls. No one has even come close. On one occasion, he stopped midway across the Falls, set up a camera on the two-inch tightrope, and took pictures while standing 170 feet above the raging waters! This was one of his many stunts. Other amazing tightrope walks across the Falls included him walking blindfolded, walking at night, walking on stilts, and even riding a bicycle across. He also walked across the Falls with a small oven attached to his back, midway stopping to cook an omelet on the oven!

As amazing as these feats were, one of his last attempts told the greatest tale of all. Monsieur Blondin mystified thousands of onlookers by crossing over the mighty rushing waters while pushing a wheel barrel, blindfolded. When he safely reached the other side, the roar of the crowd was louder than the falls themselves. Blondin quieted the crowd and asked, "Do you believe I can walk back across with a person in this wheel barrel?" The crowd roared with approval, "Yes! You're the greatest tightrope walker in the world!"

Blondin then challenged the enthusiastic crowd, "Well then, someone get in!" The crowd grew deafly silent. No one responded.

No one acted on what they believed.

In the pursuit of your dream, you will be challenged many times to put actions to your beliefs. Your obedience will be the proving factor that you *do* have faith, which is vitally important, being that the Bible says without faith it's impossible to please God.[10] When you obey, you are saying that you trust God and that you have faith that He's leading you every step of the way.

Obedience opens the way. Here's a quick newsflash. You don't have a clue of the path your life will take in the future! There's only One who does—God. No matter what comes your way, if you're a child of God, everything is working together for your good, even when it look likes pure chaos and disaster.[11] That's exactly why obedience is so important. It reveals God's plans and direction for your life.

There's a thing I call the "obedience cycle," and it goes like this. To do everything God has planned for your life will force you to a place of trust. When you trust, you obey. Obedience makes you healthy. Healthy things grow. Growing things change. Change, once again, forces you to trust.

When you trust, you obey. Obedience makes you healthy and healthy things grow! The cycle keeps moving. Don't attempt to live your dream without fully obeying the One who knows your end from the beginning. Obedience will open the divine path ordained by God.

Obedience affects those around you. The life you live isn't just for you; it's also for the ones around you and those who will come after you. Your ability to pass several obedience tests in your lifetime will not only affect your life, but those connected to you, as well.

Jonah was a man who totally disobeyed God. While he was on a boat, running from what God had told him to do, the entire ship began to rock and sink. Innocent men's lives were in grave danger all because of Jonah's disobedience. Eventually, they figured out that Jonah was going to kill them all, so overboard he went . . . and the men were saved.

In Joshua 7, the Children of Israel — the most feared army of the day — was experiencing a great defeat at the hands of Ai, a very small remnant of people. Joshua, the leader of the Israelites, went and cried out to the Lord for help. God's response wasn't what he'd expected! God said the reason they were being defeated was because of their

> **Obedience makes you spiritually healthy, but disobedience can bring death and destruction.**

disobedience. It wouldn't have made any difference if Joshua and all the leaders of Israel prayed, fasted, cried, begged, and pleaded with God until they passed out. Their defeat wasn't because of a lack of prayer; it was from a *lack of obedience*.

Other lives are hanging in the balance, relying on your obedience to God. When you obey, others are blessed and promoted.

Passing the obedience test is one of the most wonderful experiences in life, as it opens your heart and mind to what God is asking you to do. Obedience makes you spiritually healthy, but disobedience can bring death and destruction.

LIFE OR DEATH

In 1976, 106 Israelis were held hostage in a Ugandan airport by seven kidnappers who didn't understand the Israeli language. Israel sent in a tactical military team to rescue the hostages and upon entering the building, they yelled in their native language, instructing the hostages to get down and crawl. Within a few moments, all seven of the kidnappers were killed; just because they didn't understand the command. All of the hostages were rescued . . . or so they thought.

When the authorities began to take count of the survivors, they noticed three were missing. A quick check of the deceased revealed that these three were also killed during the raid. Why? Because even though they heard the command to drop and crawl, they didn't obey. Thus, they lost their lives. Were the gunmen to blame for this tragedy? No. Not obeying the orders is what actually killed the three hostages. The bullets that were meant for their enemy destroyed their own lives, simply because they didn't heed the command.

Sometimes we can think we're "too spiritual" to obey God in seemingly unimportant matters. The Bible says that people stumble because of their disobedience.[12] Let me reiterate that partial obedience doesn't count. To half-heartedly obey God with an "I'll only do what's necessary" or "I already do more than most people" attitude is not full obedience. You must pass the test all the way—with your actions and attitude.

The rewards of a life in full obedience to God are innumerable, as are the consequences for a life of disobedience. If you don't believe me, just look at the remainder of Deuteronomy 28, where

> You never give to get; you give out of obedience.

verses fifteen through sixty describe the life of the diso-
bedient. (It's interesting to note that the blessings of
obedience are listed in ten verses, while the consequences of disobedience cover fifty-three verses!) The
point is, it pays to obey.

Will God love you even if you ignore His voice and
disobey? Of course He will. His love for you is un-
changeable. However, you can be surrounded by the
love of God and still suffer the consequences brought
on by disobedience. The choice is yours.

Do you want to pass the obedience test? Then, here
are the three questions to ask yourself right now:

1. What's God asking me to do?
2. Am I completely and fully obeying what God
   has said?
3. Am I passing the obedience test with both my
   actions and attitude?

It is imperative that you pass the test.
The success to your life-dream depends on it.

Chapter 8

PROCESS OF A DREAM

Don't look now, but here's that dreaded seven-letter word again: process! As I said in the opening chapter, I haven't met many people who love going through the process of anything, especially in our microwave, "I want it, and I want it now" society. The development phase of practically anything nowadays is somewhat non-existent. It seems like to go through any type of progression in order to achieve a goal is like having all four of your wisdom teeth pulled in the same day . . . without anesthesia! But, when you stop and think about it, processes are all around us. We usually don't even recognize them. For example:

- Education is a process. First graders don't jump from the sixth grade one year to college the next.

- Maturity is a process. I don't think we will be dropping the legal driving age to eleven years old anytime soon! Why? Because maturity and responsibility are a constant developing process.

- Healing is a process. Trying to run a half marathon the week after heart surgery probably isn't in your best interest.

- Marriage is a process. If you've been married more than two years, you know this is true!

- Your computer and smart phone are each powered by a "processor" which executes every command through a programmed code.

- Success is a process. No one obtains their goals and dreams overnight. Some "overnight" successes took twenty years in the making. That's a long night!

- Health and wellness are a process. I can't begin to think of how many people I've seen sign up at a health club in January only to never darken the doors two months later. Why? Because they want the "super body" in six weeks—and that just doesn't happen!

You get the point. Processes are a part of our everyday life; yet, when it comes to something as important as living our dreams, we often look for shortcuts and ways to avoid the necessary steps to success. I can speak from experience. It's dangerous to put more emphasis on the *product* (the end result) than the *process*. While the product is what *drives* you, the process is what *makes* you.

You're becoming something greater than what you could've ever imagined.

THE GRAND DESIGN

As much as I love the buying and selling of real estate, I really enjoy the building and construction piece even more. To watch large parcels of land transform from mere dirt into a gorgeous structure is so amazing—but it never happens by happenstance or luck. There are plans and procedures that must be followed. Without these, it's not construction; it's chaos!

> While the product is what *drives* you, the process is what *makes* you.

Before one piece of dirt is moved on a construction site, an entire process of development, planning, and architectural drawings have already taken place. Now, think about what would happen if the general contractor rolled up to the construction site with the architects drawings in hand and said, "Boys, here's what we're gonna do. These plans I hold in my hands don't mean anything. I've been doing this for years, and we don't need all of these drawings. Instead, I'm just gonna tell you what to do, and we can go from there!" That, my friend, is a recipe for disaster — and probably a lawsuit!

For the structure to be correct, the construction crews must follow the carefully-designed blueprints. That's the way it works in the building process.

But, that's not all.

The exact same principle applies to building your dream.

Understand this: Your dream didn't come from you. It was placed *in* you by God — the Chief Architect of your life — before you ever took one breath of air. What does His design look like? Well, it's specific for each one of us, but His overall plan for mankind, as a whole, is pretty easy to see. Jeremiah said it this way:

> *"For I know the plans I have for you, declares the* LORD*, plans to prosper you and not to harm you, plans to give you hope and a future."*

> **Jeremiah 29:11 (NIV)**

According to this scripture, not only does God *have* a

plan; He *knows* them, as well. This means, He knows every twist and turn—every victory and every disappointment, each step forward to living your dream and every setback. You simply have to trust that God is working in you both to will and to do His good pleasure.[1] No matter where you are in the pursuit of your dream, God's at work in every step of the process . . .

. . . Even when you can't see Him.

AT WORK IN THE DARK

Long before the age of digital cameras, photography was much more complex. Unlike today, where you can store hundreds of pictures in your phone at one time and print them all on your home printer, there was a time when taking photographic images shot from a camera onto film were turned into printed pictures using a special procedure. Back in the day, it wasn't aim, click, shoot, and print; there was much more to it.

There was a process.

Most of all early photographs were developed in what was known as a "dark room." Some photographers still use this process even in our digital world. The dark room is a place where light is completely shut out, which allows light-sensitive photographic materials (called negatives) to develop smoothly into beautifully-printed pictures.

One of the benefits of using a darkroom is that no

two images ever come out quite the same. There are, however, a few challenges, as well. Mainly, it's dark; and you can't see the changes to the film happening right in front of your eyes. Photographers have to simply trust their skillset to know when a picture is fully developed.

That sounds a whole lot like the process of life at times, doesn't it? The beauty is we're all unique, but there are dark times along the trail. Times where you can't see your next step. Times where your overall vision is cloudy or lost. Times of isolation where you feel no one is committed to your dream but you. Let me tell you, in these "darkrooms" of life, God has a way of perfecting things in you that you can't see. When in the darkroom, you might not be able to see your hand in front of your face, let alone the finished product of your dream; but your Grand Designer can—and what He sees is good!

No one ever wants to go through the dark places of life. It's not fun. There's very little excitement and momentum. At times, things can seem to be digressing instead of progressing; but that's the exact place where God can do His greatest work. When you're in the "darkroom," there's a developmental process taking place. God's taking the "negatives" and changing them into something beautiful and radiant. You simply have to trust His work in progress.

How do you get through the "darkrooms" of life?

It's called blind trust. The darkroom isn't as bad as it may seem. Character is built in the darkroom. Courage is developed there. Sure, it may feel unbearable at times, but your life's Chief Architect is more focused on what you're *becoming* than what you're *doing*. The key is to be faithful and full of faith. I've heard it said before that when you can't trace God, you have to trust Him. He's working in every step of the process.

> . . . when you can't trace God, you have to trust Him.

THE END FROM THE BEGINNING

No matter how you see yourself or how others view you, God's opinion of you is the only one that matters. Regardless of what your life looks like at this moment, He sees you living His dream for your life to the fullest. It reminds me of a story in the Bible of a man named Gideon.

After Joshua led the Children of Israel into the Promised Land, the next generation rebelled against God. In response, God handed them over to their enemies. Needless to say, these were dark days for God's people, but God already had a plan of deliverance.

Gideon was a man who, like most of the Israelites at this time, was living in a state of displacement. The Bible says that the angel of Lord came and found him thresh-ing wheat in a winepress.[2] Now, this might not sound too odd, but think about the purpose of a winepress. It's used to crush grapes into wine. So, the question is, why is Gideon hiding, threshing wheat in a winepress, which is a job that was meant to be done in the open air—threshing wheat? He was full of fear.

But, that's not how God saw him.

Look how the messenger from Heaven addresses Gideon:

"The Lord is with you, mighty warrior."

Judges 6:12 (NIV)

Talk about a dichotomy! Gideon was anything BUT a mighty warrior; but God saw him as what He was created to be, not as he was in his current state.

God always sees people as they're created to be, no matter where they are in the process of life. For example, Moses was a refugee hiding in the desert when God called him to deliver His people from Egypt.[3]

Before Abraham ever had a son, God called him the "father of many nations."[4]

The angel called Mary "blessed and highly favored" before she was even pregnant with Jesus.[5]

In the same way, God sees you living in the fullness your dream, right now, even though you can't see it.

On the journey to your dream, there will be times where you won't feel like the strongest, the most accomplished, the most talented, or even the most successful person in the world. Anyone who has ever lived their life-dream walks through those same seasons. When you find yourself in that position, keep your head up! Always remember that no matter how you may see yourself, *it's not what God sees*. He sees the end from the beginning!

And that's all that matters.

FOUR POINTS

Are you at a place where you see yourself as losing ground or not making the progress you desire? Has your enemy, the devil, been shouting in your mind thoughts of defeat and failure; and it's affected your self-perception? Are you having a hard time seeing yourself as capable of living your dream to the fullest? I can assure you that if you're not dealing with these types of issues now, somewhere along the way, you will. When you do and giving up seems eminent, remember these four tips:

1. **You're doing better than you think you are**. Maybe you're not where you thought you'd be at this point of the process, but you're better than when you started. No matter where you

are right now, always remember that God sees you complete. The devil will always tell you that you'll never make it; but at the end of the day, God's plan will have the last word.

2. **You're stronger than you think you are.** If you're a born-again Christian, then think for a moment what's on the inside of you — the DNA of Jesus! Your spirit-man is full of the same Spirit that raised Jesus from the dead. God's supernatural strength is constantly working in you. Even when you're weak, you're still winning; for it's there that God's strength is made perfect.[6]

3. **You matter more than you think you do.** You were not put on this earth by accident. God created you ON purpose and FOR a purpose. Before you were ever conceived, God knew everything about you, and He knew His divine plan for your life.[7] In hard times, keep your focus on the One who made you and has designed you for greatness.

4. **You're closer than you think you are.** Like me, you've probably always heard the saying, "Keep your eyes on the prize." While that may sound like a good thing, it's not always

the best choice. If your happiness relies upon reaching your end result, then your enemy will do everything possible to keep you from arriving at your destination. Keep your joy in the journey, and you'll come to see how close you really are to living your dream.

THE MAJORITY

There are many moments and seasons in the process of your dream where everything clicks, the momentum is high, and you feel practically invincible. We all LOVE those times and wish we could stay there forever! However, those pockets of time are only a part of your journey. There are other facets of the process you'll have to face that aren't nearly as much fun – at least, not in the beginning. However, in the end, they move you closer to your destiny. Let's look once again at the story of Gideon, as he faced one of these trying moments.

Gideon's destiny was laid out before him: to deliver the Israelites from their enemies. Knowing how many armies he would need to defeat his enemies, Gideon did what any one of us would've done – he rallied the troops. Answering the call were 32,000 soldiers. Gideon had to be ecstatic, but God wasn't so impressed. Gideon's success wasn't going to be dependent on his recruiting skills, but rather how much he could trust God with his life. That trust was about to be put to the test.

When God saw the number of men gathered, He told Gideon something no one who is pushing toward their dream wants to hear: "Gideon, you have too many people! Everyone who is full of fear, send them home."[8] Not only did he have too many—at least, from God's perspective—Gideon had also recruited the wrong type of people. He obeyed God's command and in a blink of an eye, Gideon lost 10,000 soldiers! Can you imagine the look on his face as he watched thirty percent of his team walk away?

The process was just beginning.

Then, God instructed Gideon to take those who remained down to the brook for a drink of water. That sounds like a nice gesture, but it was more than just a water break; it was a test. How the soldiers drank their water would be the sign of who stayed and who was sent home. Those who lapped the water like a dog had to go. Those, who got down on a knee and using their cupped hands to scoop up the water to their mouths, stayed. After the test was completed, another 21,700 of Gideon's soldiers were removed. In the end, only 300 men, from the original 32,000 were left to fight. That was 31,700 soldiers who were sent home. Talk about a test of faith! No matter how many were sent back, Gideon was about to find out this truth: *He and God were a majority!*

Gideon and his mighty army of 300 men defeated every army who was an enemy to Israel. What he came to realize was that the process to victory was never about the *number of men*, but rather the *spirit of faith* that was in them. Gideon learned a valuable lesson that day, that fear and faith can never cohabitate. One has to be removed for the other to work. God had a plan for Gideon and his army the entire time; but for the dream to be fulfilled, he had to trust the process.

Gideon had to let things go.

LET IT GO!

Leann and I have never been like Gideon—heading to war with a small remnant of soldiers—but we've experienced a very similar situation where, in order to move into what God had prepared for us, something had to go. It wasn't easy, but the end result made the pain of "losing" something all worth it.

After we had sold our "dream" house out in the country, we needed a place to live. A subdivision, close to the church, caught our eye when we very first moved to Forney. It just so happened that at the time we needed to move, a friend of ours had a house in that subdivision for lease. Leann really liked the house (which is a vitally important factor for a happy marriage), so we came into a lease/purchase agreement with the owner. We would lease it for a year and then purchase the home outright for a set price.

One of the things that got our attention about this particular house was a gorgeous chandelier in the formal dining area. I told the owner that since we were leasing for a year, we would like to purchase the chandelier and own it outright. He agreed, so I wrote him a check. Everything was set . . . or so it seemed.

One year later, our lease was coming to an end, and we were positioned to purchase the house according to the price in the original contract. It was a very simple process, until we hit a snag. When we met with the owners to finalize the transaction, they said, "We know we agreed on a price a year ago, but we're going to need $20,000 more than what the contract says." I didn't know whether to faint or jump across the table! After some discussion, there was no other option left but for us to move . . .

. . . But the chandelier was coming with us!

Seeing that the owners had already defaulted on our original agreement, I felt it necessary to remind them about our purchase of this chandelier and that it would be coming with us. Immediately, he responded, "Oh, no, that chandelier is staying with the house." At that point, I was about ready to lose my salvation! I said, "Sir, I wrote you a check to buy it, and I have a copy of the check in my files." He said, "No, you didn't buy it, you *rented it from us for a year!*"

As much as it pained me at the time, I knew this was an argument I wasn't going to win. Not only were we being forced to leave the home we had planned on buying, but now the chandelier (which we had already bought and paid for) was staying, too. Nothing about this transaction was right, but we put it in God's hands and walked away.

We had to let it go.

A few months later, I drove back through the very same subdivision to see if any homes were for sale. Much to my surprise, the builder was selling the model home, which sat at the very front of the subdivision. I thought to myself, *"Hey, it can't hurt to go in and see what what they're selling it for."* So, I did.

This model home was fully decked out with the best features and upgrades, plus a house full of furniture and custom window draperies. I figured since they were selling the house, then why not offer to buy everything that was already in it? The salesperson gave me a price for the house plus all of the custom furniture and fixtures. I immediately counter-offered an amount far below what she said. We went through a time of negotiations and finally agreed on a price for the house and all of the furniture—for almost $100,000 lower than the original asking price!

. . . fear and faith can never cohabitate.

That was only the beginning of the story.

After we finalized the deal, I went and picked up Leann and said, "I have something to show you." We drove straight to the house where I told her, for the first time, that we had just bought it! I wasn't quite sure how she would react, but what she said blew my mind. Moving over to the staircase where we could have a little privacy, she said, "Richie, I've never told you this, but when we first moved here two years ago, I walked into this very same house and fell in love with it. I knew it would be ours one day. I walked over and stood at the bottom of this same stairway and prayed, '*Lord, one day, they will sell this house. This is my dream home, and I would appreciate it if you could make a way for us to buy it,*' and now we own it!"

Today, we still live in Leann's dream home.

Now, look at how the process all worked out. Had we not been forced to move, we wouldn't have been ready to purchase this home when it came available. In the heat of the moment, it looked as though we were losing and taking a giant step backwards; but God knew the end from the beginning! The test wasn't walking away from the house as much as it was us leaving the chandelier. Oh, yeah, you better believe I wanted to jump in that house many times after we had moved and take it down, but something greater than a light fixture was at stake. To live in our dream home, we had to let the chandelier go. It wasn't easy to do, but we learned that it was all part of the process.

NOT WHAT YOU SEE

When things aren't happening at the speed you would

like them to, you have to trust the process. You might not be able to see the finished product quite yet, but God sees it. He's very capable of showing you the entire thing, but the magnitude might scare you away. The Bible says if you love God, then your eye has not seen, your ear has not heard, nor have all the things that God has prepared for you even entered into your heart.[9] Even if it's good now, just wait—the best hasn't even begun!

Since we started the church, I've dealt with so many days of frustration. Even though I'm so thankful for how far we've come and where we are today, I really thought we would be double our current size right now. Just when I start to look at all the things we don't have, I remember what stage of the process we're in, and it quickly changes my perspective.

The truth is we couldn't handle a congregation twice our size right now, as we aren't in the position to properly manage, develop, and grow. We would be in over our heads, drowning in our "success," and running full speed just to stay ten steps behind! As frustrating as it can be at times, I have to trust that the process of our development and growth is preparing us to ultimately enter into God's very best. The Great Architect is still at work!

What do you do when your present situation doesn't look anything like the finished plan? Be faithful to the process! When you fail to trust the development of things in and around you, the temptation to quit will overwhelm you and you might not ever see the finished product. Thomas Edison said it this way:

> "Many of life's failures are people who did not realize how close they were to success when they gave up."

Never give up on your dream because of one setback. Doing so would be like slashing three of your tires because the fourth one is flat! You don't fight one battle, and then your life is over. As long as you live, you'll be fighting to keep your dream alive. If nothing else, you'll have to fight discouragement, sometimes daily.

Trust in the Lord, that He is working everything out for your good. His grand design is to bless you, prosper you, and to give you a hope and a future. Always keep your dream alive! Most importantly, keep pressing forward and always remember: The dream is a process.

Enjoy the journey.

Chapter 9

THE POWER OF POTENTIAL

Don't you wish that, at least on occasion, you could push the "pause" button on life like you can on your DVR or TiVo® recorder? Well, just for a minute, imagine that you can put your life on pause mode. Now, step back a few steps and look at what you see. Look at where you've been, what you've accomplished, and where you are right now. Are you happy with what is showing in that still frame? Are you at the pinnacle of your dream, or are you somewhere in the journey? Now, a hard question: While looking at this picture, is your dream nowhere in sight? No matter what you see — ultimate success and victory or seemingly defeat and disaster — I have great news for you . . .

There's still more in you than
what's already come out of you!

It's called the power of potential. The question is, "What are you going to do with it?"

One of the worse things a forty year-old professional athlete can ever hear is, "You have great potential!" At that age, they don't care about what they could've or should've done. Sadly, the truth is, if you don't use what God has given you, every day, then you'll wind up in the "could've, should've, would've" crowd. That's not God's best for your life. There's more in you than meets the eye.

In his book, *Year to Success*, author and multi-millionaire (at twenty-nine years old), Bo Bennett, said something very powerful:

> "Every day, people settle for less than they deserve. They are only partially living or at best living a partial life. Every human being has the potential for greatness."

Let's look at this word, "potential," for a moment. It comes from the root word, "potent." When something is considered potent, it means it has great power, influence, or effect. In order for a drug to be effective, it must be potent. For a chemical to be explosive, it must be potent. If a woman is going to reproduce life, she must be impregnated by a male who is potent. Things that are potent represent great potential.

Go back with me for a moment back to your junior

high science class. You probably learned a term called "potential energy." If you don't remember exactly what that means, let me give you a quick refresher. Potential energy is stored within an object which is *capable of becoming active*. That, my friend, is you! You're a huge bundle of potential energy just waiting to be released and become active. It's time you do something about it.

It's time for your *potential* to come alive and make a difference in your life!

TURN IT INTO SOMETHING GREAT

What turns potential energy into kinetic (moving) energy is simply one thing: motion. A rubber band that's stretched to its limits has only potential energy. But, when it's released and is set in motion, then its potential comes alive. The same is true in life. You are full of God-given potential; but for it to become effective, something must be put into motion.

You must *do* something.

One of the final words Jesus spoke before leaving this earth was the word, "Go." (Isn't it interesting that two-thirds of God is "Go!") Jesus said, *"Go into all the world and preach the gospel to every creature."*[1] In essence, what Jesus told His disciples was simple: "Take what you have in you (their potential) and put legs to it! *Go.* Do something. Put the greatness in you into motion and watch what I will do!" That's still what He's saying today. Your life-dream will never come to pass by you sitting around doing nothing. You must take action, make some headway, and turn your potential into something that's moving and dynamic.

Inside of you lies so much power, so much authority, and so much future! If you don't believe it, then look at what the Apostle Paul told his son in the faith, Timothy. He told him to *stir up the gift of God that was in him.*[2] We always get excited about the stirring up part, but look where that gift is located. It's IN YOU! John said that *"Greater is he that is IN YOU than he that is in the world."*[3] The potential to do every single thing God has called you to do is already IN YOU; it's just waiting to be activated.

Now, it's time to "Go" and turn it into something great.

Maybe you've done exactly this, and today you're living your dream. If so, let me give you a word of caution: Your enemy would love to make you think that you've already accomplished everything you can, and that now it's time to sit back, relax, and enjoy your successes; but that's a trap. Maybe things are good in your life, but is that God's best for you? Best-selling author, Jim Collins, said that the biggest enemy to being *great* is being satisfied with being *good.* Don't settle for "good." No matter what you've accomplished, it may be just the tip of the iceberg. Don't limit God. There's more inside of you.

A BLENDED FORCE

A few years ago, a news article really caught my attention. In 2011, Miami Dade County officials noticed a significant rise in the population of the African rock python snake, which caused great alarm. These larger-than-life snakes can grow to lengths in excess of fifteen feet long; and in their native homeland, they've been known to eat goats and crocodiles! (Just for the record, a snake that is fifteen inches long is too big for me!) Over a three-day search, authorities found five of these snakes loose—one which was fourteen feet long and one that was thirty-one inches in circumference. But, the size of these creatures wasn't their main concern.

Officials were more worried that these African rock pythons would begin to mate with another breed of snake called the Burmese python. At this time, the Burmese python had already established a foothold in the Everglades; but with the African rock python now on the loose, the concern of a hybrid snake was frightening. Individually, these two breeds of snakes were dangerous; but when bred together, the

> The potential to do every single thing God has called you to do is already IN YOU; it's just waiting to be activated.

potential of what they could reproduce was enormous. Actually, it's downright scary! The county officials gave this blend a name:

The "super snake!"

Even though I'm not even remotely interested in snakes, this whole scenario really made me think. Without a doubt, there's unlimited potential inside of you; but what vast effectiveness could you have if you began to develop an intimate relationship with Jesus? What could happen if your sporadic prayer time moved into a daily communion with God? What would happen if you traded dead religion for a thriving, living, active relationship with the Creator of the Universe? Can you imagine the impact you could have by actually cultivating intimacy with your Heavenly Father? Not only would it impact you, but it would greatly affect those who follow after you — and *that's* what scares your enemy, the devil.

Just as the Florida officials feared the reproduction of the "super snake," the devil isn't afraid of you being a Christian all by yourself. His greatest fear is you becoming intimate with Jesus and then reproducing yourself and making disciples . . . who will reproduce themselves . . . who will reproduce themselves . . . and so on.

Several years ago, Pastor Cesar Castellanos in Bogota, Columbia began sharing the Gospel in his home with twelve people. For the longest time, they never grew past this number. But, eventually, those twelve brought twelve, who then brought twelve, and so on. Soon, they grew to 144 in attendance, then to 1,728, then to 20,000; and today, Pastor Castellanos's church, Mission Charismatic International, has over 200,000 members! This is the powerful potential that is lethal to your enemy.

The two greatest commandments Jesus gave us was to love God and to love people.[4] Knowing this, where do you think your enemy is going to attack you the most? It's in your relationships . . . with God and with others. He knows those relationships will reproduce and cause the most damage to his kingdom.

It's time to release our full potential.

ADVERSITY

I would like to say that developing your God-given potential is an easy, made-to-order formula that never includes setbacks, disappointments, or adversity; but that's not the truth. Many times, you find what's inside of you during trials and battles. It's been said for years that life is the hardest teacher, as it gives you the tests first and the lessons later. How true this is. I once heard a great analogy on this subject, using the pattern of a song.

Have you ever noticed how the chorus of a song will almost always stay the same, but the verses are different? The same is true with your life-song. If your life was a song, the chorus would be the same: God is faithful; but the verses would all be different. It might flow something like this:

Verse one: I went through hardship.

Chorus: God is faithful.

Verse two: I was given a devastating report by the doctors.

Chorus: God is faithful.

Verse three: I had to file bankruptcy.

Chorus: God is faithful.

Verse four: My spouse left me and my children.

Chorus: God is faithful.

No matter what the circumstances, that's the way your life-song is constructed. Now, with that in mind, take this into consideration:

> When you face ad-versity, God is simply
> ADD-ing another VERSE to your life!

. . . And the song goes on . . . God is faithful!

Truett Cathy, the founder of Chick-fil-a® restaurants found this to be true. Not only did one of his first restaurants burn to the ground, but he also lost two brothers that same year in a tragic plane crash, one being his business partner. Still, Mr. Cathy pressed through seemingly unsurmountable hardship and today, Chick-fil-a® operates 1,400 stores worth billions of dollars, but he's far from the only one.

Henry Ford went bankrupt five times before building an automotive empire right in the middle of the Great Depression. Walt Disney was fired from a newspaper because he "lacked imagination and had no good ideas." Later, Anaheim, California rejected his proposal for Disneyland® on numerous occasions because, in their eyes, it would only attract riff-raff. Still, Walt Disney moved forward, developed, and released his potential, and went on to not only prove the city of Anaheim (and the world, for that matter) wrong, but he built yet another empire, Disney World®, out of a swamp in central Florida.

Who else walked through adversity to greatness? Abraham Lincoln came from poverty to riches, only to file bankruptcy, and then became one of the greatest presidents of all time. Donald Trump experienced several bankruptcies on his way to world-renowned fortune. William Durant found himself broke on numerous occasions prior to starting General Motors® and Chevrolet®. No matter the setback, it was just another verse to these men's story.

From 1967 to 2008, the New Orleans Saints had only experienced five winning seasons. Not only had they endured one of the worse franchise records in all of professional sports, but their city was devastated by Hurricane Katrina in 2005 to the point where they played no home games that season. In 2006, they took a gamble on a quarterback who had experienced what most considered a career-ending shoulder injury. The results? In 2009, that same quarterback, Drew Brees, led the Saints to their first world title; plus, he was chosen as the Super Bowl MVP!

You might not be Abraham Lincoln, Walt Disney, or Drew Brees, but that doesn't matter. God knows exactly who you are and where you are right now. The Bible says that He shows no partiality.[5] What He has done for others, He will do and work for you! You are special. You are called. You are gifted by God — and you're not finished.

You're loaded with potential just waiting to burst out.

WALK IT OUT

People have asked me on several occasions, "Richie, how do I turn the potential of my dream inside of me into something productive?" I believe turning your potential into unbelievable, world-class results boils down to a few, simple foundations.

> **Be a doer**. Let me reiterate that *motion* turns potential energy into results! You have to be a doer of what God has placed inside of you. Get up and get moving. It's one thing to have faith that God has given you a dream, but it's an entire different thing to put *action* to your faith. Look at how nineteenth century, French poet and philosopher,

Paul Valery, stated it:

> "The best way to make your dreams come true
> is to wake up."

If you sit around and wait for "something to happen," you'll will be waiting until you die! The book of James tells us not to be mere hearers, but to actively do what we've heard.[6] When you become a doer, you'll discover your platform and begin to release your potential.

Be a doer.

Don't quit. By now, you're probably sick of reading "Don't quit!" That's okay. Someone needs to be telling you that on a daily basis, so it might as well be me! The great Christian patriarch, Leonard Ravenhill, once said:

> "Christians believe to the point of
> inconvenience."

How correct he was. Most people can believe God, until it becomes an inconvenience, . . . and then they quit. Subsequently, they miss out on God's best for their lives. The choice is yours: You can be a part of something great or quit and hear about it later. Never, ever quit. Keep dreaming and keep believing!

Make a commitment. Best-selling author and business mogul, Brian Tracy, said:

> "There is no real limit to how much better a
> person who really commits to getting better
> can be."

No one ever maxes out their full potential—no one. Even the greatest can still be better. It all comes down to what you are willing to commit to. Look at it this way. Every time you sit down to a bacon and egg breakfast, let it remind you that the chicken *contributed* to that meal; but the pig, he was *committed*! Develop a stick-to-it attitude that cannot be moved. Be driven by your dream and watch the potential in you produce more than you could've ever imagined. Make a commitment and stick to it no matter what.

What God has designed for you will blow your mind. Don't limit Him. The sky is not the limit; there are no limits with God. Grow through adversity. Never settle for where you are. Even if it's amazing, it can still be better and more effective. Be a doer. Don't quit. Commit for the long haul. Your potential is ready to be released.

And, it's more than you could've ever imagined!

Chapter 10

SIGNS OF GRACE

Tuesday, May 13, 2014, was a day that changed my life forever. A day I knew would eventually come, but wasn't quite ready to accept when it happened so suddenly. A day that seemed to be the worst day in my life. Yet, it has become a pivotal, defining moment for my future. A day I will never forget.

It was the day my dad, my life hero, passed away.

While every message we received was loving and encouraging, one phrase kept standing out to me in a very unique way: "We are so sorry for your loss." Even though I've heard and even sympathized with people using this very same message, something about it didn't seem right. In my mind, the word "loss" didn't properly describe my situation.

True, my dad had passed away, but had I really "lost" him? I didn't think so. Why? Because when you lose something, you don't know where it is! I can lose my keys, my wallet, or my car in the mall parking lot (at least temporarily); but, with Dad, I hadn't lost him based on one simple fact: I knew EXACTLY where he was . . . in Heaven with Jesus! He simply left this earth and moved into his eternal home, which really means he didn't "die," as we think. Quite the contrary. My dad is more alive today than he's ever been in his entire life!

A MAN'S MAN

All my life, I remember my dad being what's called a "man's man." There wasn't a sissy bone in his body. I've never known him to back down from a challenge or walk away from a test. He was the hardest-working man I've ever known and the most determined. No matter what anyone said, when he made up his mind concerning a matter, he was going to do whatever it took to see it through. Period. No one or nothing was going to stop him! That's one of the many attributes I loved and inherited from him.

My dad was our whole neighborhood's dad. All my friends loved him and my mom, and they always wanted to come over to our house. We were one of the very few houses who had an in-ground pool, and my parents always made everyone feel right at home. Many times, Dad would show up unannounced, load up me and my friends in the back of his pick-up truck (back when it was legal to do so), and then he would take us all to a

Braves game! You never knew what he was going to do next.

Dad was a tireless worker, which is where I learned my work ethic. For over twenty years, he worked as an hourly employee for General Motors®, twelve hours a day, six days a week. He never was afraid to work and provide for his family. We lived in a nice home, drove nice cars, and took nice vacations. Dad even managed to pay off mine and my sister's college education. The way he provided for us was a true reflection of how much he loved and believed in us. Now that I'm older and have three children of my own, I realize that the most amazing thing about dad's work ethic really wasn't how much he worked; it was how he could work so many hours and still carve out time and energy for my sister and me.

More times than I can remember, Dad would come home from a long day at work (even though he never showed any signs of tiredness or fatigue) and say, "Hey, Rich, let's go to the Braves game tonight! It's early, and they don't start until 7:40; so we have time to get there." That was always music to my ears. Even though it was just a baseball game to me, I now see it was so much more than just a game to him; it was the dedication of a great man to his family.

Everything my sister and I were involved in, Dad was right there with us. He coached my baseball teams, made sure we always had rides to and from events, was our biggest cheerleader in games, etc. I remember one time he even volunteered to coach my basketball team — and he knew absolutely NOTHING about basketball! His knowledge (or lack) of the game wasn't the issue; there was need, and he filled it. That's just the way he was.

Until his later years.

THE LAST YEARS

In the later years of my dad's life, his health rapidly declined. In some respects, it felt as though I was watching him die even while he was still alive. Crippling arthritis — a type stronger than Rheumatoid — began to overtake his body. The pain was so severe that General Motors® forced him to take an early retirement, which was a huge blow to his working man's psyche. Up until this point, he was rarely ever sick; but now that he wasn't able to work, something in him died . . . and never fully came back to life.

Dad's doctors were very concerned with his condition and did everything they could to help control his pain. They prescribed him quite a large inventory of medications; and while their intentions were good, the outcome was vastly the opposite. Here this "man's man" was now sitting around the house, depleted of emotional and physical strength, doing everything he could to make it day-to-day with the least pain as possible.

The medications that made his life more manageable became much more than pain control . . .

. . . They became an addiction.

Even with his crippling condition, the doctors called him "a man of steel!" They couldn't believe he was still alive, considering all the medications he had been taking for years. To go along with the arthritis, Dad was also a diabetic but hardly ever took insulin shots. In the end, the doctors said that because his blood sugar count was so high, it was nothing short of a miracle that he didn't lapse into a diabetic coma and die. The "man of steel" began experiencing a crack in his physical armor, as was his emotional state of mind.

While Dad wasn't the man I'd always known him to be, one thing never changed: He was still as bullheaded as always, especially when it came to his right to drive an automobile. No matter how much we tried to talk him out of it, he wouldn't listen and would literally fight anyone who tried to stop him from driving. His mind was made up; he was going to drive until the day he went to Heaven, which is exactly what happened.

MAY 13, 2014

This particular Tuesday morning started out like any other day for Dad. His customary routine was to rise early and drive fifteen minutes west of their house to start off his day by fishing in my grandfather's pond. However, this day was different. The routine was about to change.

Instead of driving his usual route just a few miles *west*, Dad took off that morning and drove east. I truly believe something made him drive the complete opposite direction, which I'll explain a little later in this chapter. It would wind up being one of our signs of grace from God.

While driving east on Interstate 20, about an hour and a half away from his house, Dad's heart literally exploded in his chest. In one breath, he stepped out of this world into eternity. He lost control of his car, slammed into an embankment, and eventually struck a tree. The good news for us was that, according to the medical reports, Dad never even knew he had been in an accident. He was with Jesus before his car hit anything.

That day is burned in my memory forever. Doubts, questions, and regrets always seem to accompany times like these. One of the things which worked on my mind and emotions the most was the thought that I never had

> **In one breath, he stepped out of this world into eternity.**

a chance to say good-bye. I'd just seen my dad three weeks prior, too. Had I known it was the last time I would see him face-to-face, there are so many things I would've told him. Who knew it would be our last time together?

God did, and He had already

prepared me for this day.

The next few weeks, I spent some time reflecting over the last month of my dad's life here on earth. I started to see how the Lord so beautifully orchestrated his every move. In His infinite wisdom, God knew I would need answers and comfort far beyond what anyone could give me. I firmly believe that not only did God know my dad was going to pass from this earth, but He also knew exactly what I was going to need to weather the storm. Thus, He gave me and my family signs.

I call them the signs of grace.

SIGNS

One of my favorite life-scriptures is Romans 8:28, which says:

> **"And we know that all things work together for good to those who love God, to those who are the called according to *His* purpose."**

Even though I believe this scripture with everything that's in me, I was definitely questioning its truth when I received the horrifying news about the accident. One of my first thoughts was, *"How can any good come out of this?"* At first, the clouds had no silver lining and there was no rainbow in sight. All I felt was immense hurt and pain. I've always heard that the worst hurt is the one you're going through, and at no time in my life was this any truer.

But, something else was at work, as well . . .

. . . God's amazing grace.

While I'm thankful for God's grace that saves us, I believe there are other functions of grace which merit our attention[1]. For example, not only are we saved by grace, but grace also empowers and enables us to live our daily lives. By God's grace, we can walk through tough circumstances and adverse situations and come out stronger on the other side. His grace also gives us the strength to stand up in the middle of opposition and tragedy and say, "If God be for me, who can be against me?"[2] No matter what you're going through, you can rest assured that His grace is more than sufficient for

> By God's grace, we can walk through tough circumstances and adverse situations and come out stronger on the other side.

you."[3] It's not about the thorn or the struggles; it's all about His grace!

God's timing is always impeccable. I honestly believe that if my dad had gone to Heaven a year earlier, I would've been a total nut case, mainly because of the relational unrest between the two of us. Don't get me wrong. I loved my dad dearly, but we hadn't been close over his last few years.

How grateful I am for the blatant signs of God's grace at work before he left this earth. These were God-ordained moments that sealed in our hearts he was home in Heaven!

These were our signs.

The Visit. Just three weeks before my dad graduated to Heaven, he visited us in Texas to celebrate my fortieth birthday and Easter. On this trip, it didn't take very long for us to notice that he wasn't himself—meaning, he was actually calm, nice, and easy to talk to! Leann made mention of this within the first few days of his visit, and we were all very glad for the change.

Another noticeable difference was his health. Normally, Dad was very sick during his visits and stayed in bed the majority of the time. This time was different. He was awake and felt good, so much so that one afternoon while Leann and the girls were doing school work, Dad started this loud banging noise, just to cause the girls to laugh. He then wanted to go to lunch with us all (another huge change), and we did exactly what he wanted. For the first time in a very long time, our family enjoyed a great lunch together with Dad, filled with laughs and stories. Something was definitely different.

So many good things happened during that

visit. God was definitely preparing us for what was to come. How well I remember one Sunday seeing my dad in our church auditorium, with his hands lifted as high as he could get them, praising and magnifying God. Our last days together were showered with times of peace, bonding, and fulfilling relationship. There's no doubt, his trip to Texas was one God's signs of grace.

Back Home. Dad blew us all away (in a good way) with his visit. Something was changing in him, and it continued even when he arrived back home. Another sign of God's grace working in his life was about to be on display.

Dad always loved the Lord and had even been a pastor some years back. He never left his job at GM and always served as a bi-vocational pastor. Over the years, however, his commitment to the things of God had fallen to the wayside — that is, until his trip to Texas. Just a few days after his return, Dad decided to sit down and watch Christian TV. He just so happened to tune into the Saturday broadcast of Lakewood Church with Pastor Joel Osteen. At the end of every broadcast, Pastor Joel always leads the television audience in the "sinner's prayer." That afternoon, at my grandparents' home in Anniston, Alabama, my dad prayed that prayer with Pastor Joel and rededicated his life to Jesus!

After the broadcast had concluded, he went and told my mom, "That's the best sermon I've ever heard!" (Thanks, Dad!) He then continued, "Me and the Lord had a long conversation today, and I know there's more work for me to do!" Dad was definitely having a revival of sorts in his heart. It was another sign of God's hand working in his life.

The Next Day. The very next day, which was a Sunday, Dad did something to prove his rededication and commitment to the Lord was for real. He went to church! He got up, got dressed, and went to the little country church where my mom and my grandmother had been attending for quite some time. That day, the pastor preached the absolute perfect message for my dad: "Overcoming Bitterness and Unforgiveness in Your Life." It was the next step in his renewal.

One of the biggest obstacles which hindered my father from having a full, loving relationship with Jesus was his deep-rooted anger and bitterness towards people who had hurt or wronged him. They were family members, former church members, other pastors and ministers — you name it. That Sunday morning, Dad caught the revelation that if God was going to forgive him, then he must forgive those whom he had held grudges toward for years—and he did.

Knowing that Dad carried all these hurts and pains for years has always concerned me. It never failed, whenever we would get into any conversation—regardless what the subject matter was—somewhere along the line, he would begin talking about how this person hurt him or that person did something unjust to him. These instances seemed to berate his mind and emotions so deeply that forgiveness seemed practically impossible.

But, God had another plan.

Dad came home from church that day a different man! In fact, he went and told my mom how God had dealt with him that morning, and that he was releasing ALL of his grudges and offenses. Some of those he had held for over thirty years. Was it just another good sermon that moved him to this resolve? Not hardly.

It was another sign of God's grace!

That Sunday would prove to be Dad's last time in church. Two days later, he would enter eternity. How fitting that the last sermon he ever heard was on forgiveness. As if these weren't enough to convince us that God's grace was all over my dad, they wouldn't be the last.

Two more awaited.

Final Exit. After hearing the news of the accident, our drive to Georgia was the longest, loneliest trip I can ever remember. Even though I was surrounded by the outpouring of love from friends and had the enormous comfort of Leann and our girls, nothing could replace the void I felt inside. In an instant, my hero was gone. I needed the assurance and peace of God like never before.

We arrived at my mom's and after a few hours of just being together, we started talking about the particulars of the incident. At first, it seemed so strange that Dad would be so disorientated that he would drive almost ninety miles in the complete opposite direction of his normal destination. We were all confused and perplexed, until God opened our eyes to yet another sign of his grace.

The last church Dad pastored, many years before the accident, was in the small town of Villa Rica, Georgia. The exit where he crashed — an hour and a half away from where he was supposed to be — was the exact exit for . . . you guessed it . . . Villa Rica, Georgia! Coincidence? Think again. It was another sign.

I believe that divine providence was at work that day. To me, dad had driven — conscientiously or not — to the last place where God had moved greatly in his life as a pastor. I believe he wasn't only reminiscing about the past, but that he was gearing up for what was yet to come. Somehow, he knew that his best days of ministry were in front of him, not behind him. It was yet another sign from God.

The Notes. One more definite sign of grace appeared in the most unusual place: the car my dad was driving.

The day after we arrived at my mom's, I went to the wrecker yard to retrieve any of Dad's personal belongings and essentials from his car. I was looking for his keys, his wallet, etc.; but what I found was more than I had bargained for. While quickly scanning through the car, I noticed an old sheet of paper laying in the front passenger's seat. It obviously had some meaning to my dad, so I picked it up. What was on that piece of paper blew me away. It was an old, handwritten sermon written by my dad on the armor of God! That was the last and final sign that we needed.

After reading what he had written, it was like my dad was saying, "I will overcome and live my dream; but to do so, I need to put on the whole armor of God."

That's exactly what he did.

The signs of God's amazing, unending grace over

EPHESIANS 6:11-18
Put on the whole armor of God

Paul is not just talking to the church, but is also talking to individuals of the church. The body of Christ.

Paul is saying we must put on the whole armor of God, not just part of it. The way we can do this is by walking in the Spirit. To be Christians we must continually walk & live in the Spirit.

The evil rulers are Satanic beings, the fallen angels that Satan has control over (We face a powerful army that whose goal is to defeat the church (Spiritual & Physical), But we are reminded in (Matthew 16:18) Upon this rock I will build my church and the gates of Hell will not prevail against it.

God has given the church a great tool to fight the powers of Hell with & that is the Holy Spirit.

"Not by might nor by power but by my Spirit saith the Lord."

I am reminded of the Book by Benie Hinn, Good Morning Holy Spirit. When you wake up the first thing we should say is good morning Holy Spirit what would you have me to do today. Praying should be as normal as breathing to a Christian.

Loins - Strong Belt - Truth

Satan fights with lies; sometimes the lies sounds like the truth, but only Christians have the truth that can defeat Satan's lies. Satan is a liar & father of all lies.

Breastplate - God's approval

The Breastplate covers our heart; protects it. Satan will try to tell you, that you won't make it; he will try to discourage you. But you can stand and say "Greater is He that is in me, than he that is in the world."

Shoes - Readness to Spread the Good News

Satan wants us to think it is a hopeless case & worthless idea to go out & tell people the good news. God gives us the motevation to proclaim the truth.

Shield - Faith

To protect us from Satan's fiery darts. Satan will insult us; we may have temporary set backs but God gives us the ability to see beyond our circumstances; to know victory is on the way.

Helment - Salvation

Satan wants us to doubt our salvation. He wants to completely destroy us if he can Satan knows where his finally destenation is and he wants to take all he can with him

Sword the word of God

The sword is the only offense in the armor. We must learn God's word and use it against my dad in his last days were undeniable. His visit to Texas, rededicating his heart to Jesus, the steps to forgive those he had harbored ill-will against for years, the pinpoint location of his accident, and the sermon notes which accompanied him on his last day on earth all said that God's hand was on him in a mighty way. Yes, Dad went through some dark years; but in the end, this one truth remained: My dad was, once again, in full pursuit of his dream . . . even until his last fleeting moments on this earth.

"MEMORIES"

After Dad's funeral, we stayed a couple of weeks with Mom to tie up any loose ends and to make sure she was going to be alright. I was doing very well, considering all that had happened, until we started our trip back to Texas. That's when reality raised its ugly head. I cried pretty much the entire trip back home. My tears weren't so much sorrow over losing my dad, especially after seeing all of the signs of God's hand on him. No, these tears carried a far deeper hurt.

As I mentioned before, my dad and I practically had no relationship to speak of in his later years. It's not something I'm proud of, but it's the truth. The guilt of not reaching out to him more during this time really took a toll on my emotions. I needed something to soothe the pain—I needed some reminder of our good times together. As soon as we arrived home, I went into my "man cave" and started my search.

It was there that I found my comfort.

While combing through some old pictures, I found a multiple-page, handwritten letter that Dad had given to me years ago. Now, this was Donnie Mullis, the "man's man" and the "man of steel" we're talking about here. While he did many things well, one thing he never claimed to be was a writer, especially a mushy one! There wasn't anything soft about him, . . . or so I thought. What I was about to read totally changed my perspective.

The letter was entitled "Memories," and it contained story after story of our life experiences together. Some I had forgotten over the years, seeing as they dated back to when I was only three years old. He talked about baseball games, camping trips, family vacations, even the times where I'd pushed my plastic mower across the yard, pretending to be mowing the lawn with him. (Eventually, I would get tired and dad would finish cutting the grass with me on his shoulders.) The contents of this letter blew my mind and released an ocean of emotions and tears. What it said was amazing, but something else about this letter was even more fascinating — when it was written.

Dad didn't write this letter after I had graduated from college, got married, had children, and was well on my way to pursuing my dream. No, he wrote it on my high school graduation night and read it that night in front of all my friends, including my girlfriend at the time. I remember him getting all choked up and emotional as he read it. I was thinking, *"Dad, can you please stop doing this in front of all my friends?"* How embarrassing it was at the time; but twenty-one years later, the truth of that letter would come to fruition: It was never written for my graduation night; it was written for me to read when my dad would be in Heaven.

It was yet another sign of God's grace at work.

CHASED BY GRACE

I realize this book isn't a memoir of the life and times of Richie Mullis, but there's something about God's grace in the midst of tragedy that's so incredible. This entire book has been dedicated to helping you recognize, develop, and live your dream — and this chapter is no different.

Maybe one of your life dreams is to reconcile a relationship with a family member, a loved one, or a close friend. That, my friend, is one of the most important dreams anyone could ever have. I know. I came painfully close to having to live with the deepest of regrets. Thank God for His grace.

If part of your dream is to reconcile relationships, let me encourage you to never give up on that dream — never. There were many times and many years where I wanted to give up on my dad. He turned into a person that I didn't even know, and it would've been so easy to cast him aside and write him off as an old, bitter, hard-nosed man who didn't care about anyone but himself. But, that wasn't the real Donnie Mullis. No matter what I saw on the outside, somewhere on the inside — buried beneath all the hurt, disappointment, and bitterness — lived the strong, caring, loving, compassionate, man of God I'd always known. It just needed to resurface.

My family and I never stopped praying for my dad, even though our relationship was strained. Before he went to Heaven, we watched God miraculously bring him out of the darkness which plagued his life for years. The entire time we were praying, God was chasing Dad down with His grace.

In the end, grace won.

As you pursue your dream, you'll find out that more people are attracted to your experiences through pain than they are your gifts and talents. No matter what you go through in the quest to live your dream, God will always be with you. Keep your eyes open. Constantly watch for His signs of grace. They're all around you; and when it's all said and done, just like with my dad, grace will win. I'm a living testimony.

Grace always wins!

Dream on.

ABOUT THE AUTHOR

Richie Mullis is the founder and lead pastor of FreeLife Church in Forney, Texas. He, along with his wife, Leann, reside in Forney with their three beautiful girls: Sydni, Ashtyn, and Eden.

In February 2004, with only a dream and a God that fulfills dreams, Richie and Leann, and their three daughters moved to Dallas to birth a new church. Since then, FreeLife has experienced amazing growth and become a beacon of hope in northeast Dallas.

Richie is committed to seeing others grow into becoming fully devoted followers of Christ. His goal is to spend the rest of his life bringing restoration, healing, and hope to the world . . . one life at a time.

Richie Mullis

FreeLife Church
P.O. Box 2007
Forney, TX 75126

Visit us online:
freelifechurch.org

Phone:
972.552.3344
972.639.4259

E-mail:
pastorrichie@freelifechurch.org

Follow Richie on Social Media:
Facebook.com/RichieMullis

ENDNOTES

Chapter 1: CALLING ALL DREAMERS
1. Genesis 37:19.
2. 2 Kings 2:9-10.
3. Galatians 6:7.
4. John 10:10.
5. 1 John 4:4.

Chapter 2: TWO SIMPLE WORDS
1. www.sba.gov/sites/default/files/FAQ_Sept_2012.pdf. September 2012.
2. Ibid.
3. U.S. Census Bureau 2012.
4. Ibid.
5. Organization for Economic Co-operation and Development.
6. New York Times, August, 2010.
7. Hebrews 12:2.
8. Philippians 1:6.

Chapter 4: THE MIRACLE OF EMPTINESS
1. Exodus 4:2-3.
2. Zechariah 4:6.
3. 1 Kings 18:44.
4. Matthew 7:11 and Luke 6:38.
5. John 3:30.
6. Mark 14:3-5.

Chapter 5: STIRRING THE WATERS
1. Revelation 1: 10-11.
2. Revelation 2:1, 8, 12, 18; 3:1,7, 14.
3. Mark 10:47.

4. Mark 10:48.
5. Romans 12:15.

Chapter 6: DIVINE COUNTERBALANCE
1. *Strong's Exhaustive Concordance* word # 2218.
2. Genesis 50:20 (Paraphrased).
3. Job 2:9.
4. Revelation 1:18.
5. 1 Corinthians 15:55.
6. Psalms 30:5 (paraphrased).
7. Psalms 34:19 (paraphrased).
8. Proverbs 24:16.
9. John 18:10.
10. Luke 22: 54-62.
11. Matthew 16:21-23.
12. John 21:15-17.
13. Acts 2:41.
14. Acts 5:15.
15. 2 Corinthians 5:7.

Chapter 7: PASSING THE TEST
1. 2 Chronicles 7:14.
2. Luke 6:38.
3. Matthew 7:7.
4. 1 John 1:9.
5. Genesis 22:12 (NIV).
6. Philippians 2:8.
7. Luke 22:42.
8. Philippians 2:9 (NIV).
9. Matthew 25:21-23.
10. Hebrews 11:6.
11. Romans 8:28.
12. 1 Peter 2:8.

Chapter 8: THE PROCESS OF A DREAM

1. Philippians 2:13.
2. Judges 6:11.
3. Exodus 3:10.
4. Genesis 17:4.
5. Luke 1:28 (Paraphrased).
6. 2 Corinthians 12:9.
7. Psalms 139:13-16.
8. Judges 7:2-3 (Paraphrased).
9. See 1 Corinthians 2:9.

Chapter 9: THE POWER OF POTENTIAL

1. Mark 16:15.
2. 2 Timothy 1:6.
3. 1 John 4:4.
4. Luke 10:27.
5. Acts 10:34 (KJV).
6. James 1:22.

Chapter 10: SIGNS OF GRACE

1. Ephesians 2:8.
2. Romans 8:31 (Paraphrased).
3. 2 Corinthians 12:9.